Carl Auer

Roswita Königswieser/
Martin Hillebrand

Systemic Consultancy in Organisations

Concepts – Tools – Innovations

In cooperation with Johann Ortner
Translated from the German by Angela Dickinson

2005

Published by Carl-Auer-Systeme Verlag: www.carl-auer.de

Carl-Auer-Systeme Verlag
Häusserstr. 14
69115 Heidelberg

Coverdesign: Goebel/Riemer
Layout: Verlagsservice Josef Hegele, Dossenheim
Printed in Germany
Printed by: Freiburger Graphische Betriebe
www.fgb.de
First edition, 2005
ISBN 13: 978-3-89670-499-3
ISBN10: 3-89670-499-0

Title of the original edition:
„Einführung in die systemische Organisationsberatung“

Bibliographic information published by Die Deutschen Bibliothek
Die Deutsche Bibliothek lists this publication
in the Deutsche Nationalbibliografie; detailed bibliographic
data is available in the Internet at http://dnb.ddb.de.

Contents

Preface

Only a few years ago, it would have been very difficult to even imagine writing an introduction to systemic organisational consulting for a wide readership from a range of different professions. In the meantime, this previously well-kept secret has emerged from its niche existence to become an infinitely presentable and attractive approach to organisational consulting in both the profit and non-profit sectors. Systemic training programmes continue to boom as change managers and conventional consultants alike look increasingly to this form of consulting when traditional methods fail.

However, learning and adopting the systemic approach is by no means easy, since it is ultimately a question of attitude and thus involves far more than simply know-how that can be taught and learned. Our many years of experience both as consultants and trainers have shown us not only how difficult systemic organisational consulting can be to learn, but also how effective it can be.

We would also like to make clear that the aim of this book is to present *our* approach to systemic consulting and that we lay no claims to this being either the only or the only correct approach to systemic organisational consulting.

The objectives of this introductory guide to systemic consulting posed an enormous challenge. Its intent is not only to illustrate the complexities, intricacies and multiple meanings of this approach, but also to deliver a clear insight into the praxis of systemic organisational consulting and into the actual methods and intervention possibilities used. At the same time, we also wanted to provide the reader with some guidelines and typical examples, offering a taste of systemic "reality", illustrating how difficult systemic consulting can be (and indeed usually is) and highlighting the stumbling blocks that may be encountered on the way.

To give readers – be they consultants, project managers, students or simply anyone with an interest in the subject – an impression of our day-to-day work, we begin our trip into the chaotic and exciting world of systemic organisational consulting with an example of an actual consulting project. This case study embraces all the different elements that go to make up this approach[I]: an adventurous journey with all the associated highs and lows. Whilst this gives an impression of the region, the countryside, the people and their customs, it nonetheless remains only a travelogue and cannot replace the actual experience itself.

We then take a short detour to the origins of systems theory and introduce some of the key terms used in systemic organisational consulting. In doing so, we use our case study to create the link to the three main levels of system intervention and the five dimensions that need to be considered at each of these levels.

Continuing with our travel analogy, these three intervention levels – architecture, design and tools – can be compared to a guide book: they provide basic guidelines, recommended routes, tools, "rules of thumb" and checklists on what to pack. To accompany our journey, we have included a selection of interventions that are both relevant to the case study yet also highlight issues that have not previously been described in detail in other publications[2].

We would like to extend our thanks to all the clients and colleagues we have worked with in the course of our projects and who have helped us to continually develop new ideas. We would also like to thank all the people who have participated in our training programmes for the opportunity they gave us to discuss our ideas and put our experience to the test.

Many thanks also to our fellow consultant Stephan Rey and to the design agency fenzl & conrad who provided the illustrations for this book.

Our particular thanks also go to Angela Dickinson for her precise and sensitive translation of our texts.

Finally, a very special thank you to Johann Ortner for his valuable contributions to this book and his expert help in preparing the manuscript.

Roswita Königswieser, Martin Hillebrand
Vienna/Bremen
June 2005

1. "Chance" – A Systemic Consulting Project

Over the course of our careers as consultants, we have had the good fortune to get to know, work with and come to respect many different customers and projects. When looking for a suitable example of systemic consulting to use in this book, we focused on finding a project that the reader could easily identify with and understand. We felt that large-scale consulting projects dealing simultaneously with extreme situations, restructuring, development, cultural change, vision and strategy building would be too complex and too confusing to use as case studies. However, while the interventions used in "simpler" consulting projects – such as team development projects – are easier to describe, they do not really offer sufficient depth of material and are, in any case, usually included in longer-term, more complex projects.

We finally opted for the following example: a change process spanning several years in an international group of companies. The group's core business is industrial plant manufacturing, and it has over 20,000 employees worldwide, 40 percent of whom are German-speaking. The company had excellent technical know-how, good market access and strong order levels, but corporate earnings left something to be desired. Years of politically backed monopoly status had obscured both inconsistent management policies and an organisational structure that did little to support its business processes. There was no corporate vision. Employees were resigned to the situation, and the company's market value was alarmingly low.

In addition to the hard facts, the company also had to contend with deep-seated problems of attitude and mindset. A situation of intense competition ruled between the different divisions. There was no feeling of unity, of being one company. Hierarchical structures dominated, autonomy was underdeveloped and decision-making was "political" and cumbersome. The company's general expectations of us as consultants were based on their previous experience with other consulting firms: we would either deliver a proposal for an expensive change project or claim that we could quickly untangle the "central problem".

A minority group of influential players had brought us in and accepted our terms and conditions. In the first meeting, we immediately proposed three interventions: a system diagnosis, a core group to act as the driving force behind the change process and regular coaching for the management board.

No mention was made to the client at this stage of a "systemic approach". Indeed, our recommendation that the core group include not only people "in positions of power", but also those "affected by the situation" and those "with process know-how" was greeted with astonishment. But it was met, and the ten-person core team that was formed included not only the chairman of the board, the head of the works council and management representatives, but also "ordinary workers" from the different companies in the group. The aim was to create a corporate microcosm, a group that reflected the main factions found across the company. That was why it had to include "outsiders" – critical minds and young non-conformists – not just the people whose opinions had counted most in the past, e.g. the board, the division heads and the project managers.

Throughout the book, we will present this case study primarily from the core group's perspective, since the responsibility for defining the whole process lay in their hands. Their focus on their "shared task" and, above all, the team development exercises held at the start of and throughout the project helped create stability and cohesion in the core group.

In its first meeting, the core group decided to call the project "Chance", a name that worked well in several languages. The core group met once a month, and the discussions in these one and a half day workshops were often conflict-ridden and emotional. As coaches to this group, we prepared designs for these meetings in cooperation with our colleague, Uwe Cichy, and "moderated" or intervened as necessary. The seating arrangement at these workshops – a circle of inwardly facing chairs without tables – brought the first objection: "Is this esoteric set-up really necessary?" We began by working on open issues in sub-groups, using not just cognitive or conceptual methods, but also "analogue" methods (see note 10). For example, we asked them to draw pictures in response to the following questions: What state is the company in now? What would it look like in an ideal world? The results clearly symbolised the situation, depicting the company as a "fleet of individual ships in intermittent radio contact with each other" – bleak, without orientation and grey. The "vision" pictured the whole company on board a modern ocean liner – colourful, attractive and energetic. An individual exercise designed to awaken positive images of the future had preceded the picture drawing exercise and contributed significantly to its effect.

Through its make-up, the group automatically incorporated the whole spectrum of possible perspectives ("principle of multiple perspectives") and relevant stakeholders into the process and expanded the horizons of perception of all group members.

Over time, the opinions voiced and stories told became more and more candid, and some members of the group found themselves shocked, touched and shaken by what they were hearing. For example, when a technician talked – hesitantly at first – about the way mistakes were covered up in projects and how it was impossible to introduce timely countermeasures, the response was unanimous: "If that's the way we act at the grassroots, something really has to be done."

Three core areas – soft issues – were prioritised and sub-projects set up to address them: the development of a corporate vision to serve as a guiding star and provide employees with a point of reference, measures to reduce bureaucracy and create a more efficient organisation, and internal communication. The kick-off meetings for each of these sub-projects featured both contextual and social issues.

As the project progressed, it soon became clear to all concerned that "management" was also a core issue. We began analyzing corporate management culture, for example by staging short sketches to illustrate what constituted "management today" and what should constitute "management tomorrow". The sketches not only made everyone laugh, but also triggered great concern: "We're good engineers, we have excellent professional technical and project management skills and procedures, but we aren't sensitive enough to human issues, leadership, relationships and motivation. We avoid conflicts and are afraid to talk about and learn from our mistakes. If we could change this situation, we would improve results dramatically. Our planning processes are too linear; we don't talk enough about poor development decisions or project deviations. This costs us a lot of money – we have to tackle these issues."

The use of such methods helped clarify a number of important issues. The vehement conflicts in the group regarding the change project's added value (everyone had their own picture here of who the winners and losers would be) were resolved, and the group was now ready for mutual feedback, open to our opinions and prepared to accept our interventions. Our "reflecting team" played an extremely important role in these conflict-ridden situations. The concept of two outsiders sitting down in front of the group and having a respectful, "intimate" conversation about the people present and their latent issues seemed strange at first, but soon began to have the desired effect.

Analyzing the conflicts in the management team, core group and sub-project teams helped people look at things from a wider perspective: they no longer saw things simply as black and white, but also in shades of grey. People began to recognise that everyone involved plays their own part in a problem. They stopped seeing just people and individual problems and began to notice connections, relationships and structural causes. Initially, such dialogues and discussions were strongly influenced by group dynamics and hierarchical struggles for power and position. Derogatory remarks were the order of the day. No-one listened to what their colleagues were saying; they were too busy monopolizing the conversation with long, patience-testing speeches. Often, all we could do was intervene paradoxically and use experience-oriented methods to encourage reflection.

But things did not always go smoothly. When we staged a short role-playing exercise to present the results of the vision-building process from the perspective of the relevant stakeholders, the chairman of the board stormed out of the room saying, "I've had enough of these childish games!" Everyone else remained transfixed with shock. However, slowly but surely, the reflection exercises in the core group began to have other positive effects: communication processes changed dramatically, and a great deal of energy was released into the change process. Several initiatives were launched, including the "Young Rebels" – a group founded to think laterally and speak their minds freely without restraint. They were set the task of devising a response to the following question: "If you were on the management board, what would you do to lead the company to success?"

This group's suggestions, including the introduction of joint marketing, improved business processes and consolidated human resources policies, were discussed vehemently. Some ideas were seen as very promising and, indeed, were taken up and implemented by the core group.

Although we and the two project leaders regularly encouraged the group to include profitability issues – economic indicators – in the project goals, this fell on deaf ears. As the chairman of the board commented unexpectedly: "Changing the way we think and behave will automatically bring financial rewards." Gradually, people began to accept that "hard" and "soft" factors belong together – even in projects. The introduction of a balanced scorecard was the first indication of this turnaround.

Comprehensive project reviews using learning landscapes and charts depicting highs and lows were introduced as standard practice under the motto: "learning together, not allocating blame". Before new projects were launched, stakeholder and power analyses – our standard procedure – were carried out to identify and provide a picture of the relevant stakeholders and inherent relationship and power structures. This directs attention to the building of hypotheses, opportunities and stumbling blocks. It also encourages a more careful and conscious approach: Who needs to be involved in the project? What should be our first step?

With the help of these simple tools, the importance of hypotheses became clearer, and people began to understand that there can be several different relevant points of view. As one project manager told us: "I've changed the way I think. Our technical project management with its checkboxes and rules is simply not enough. I always tried to compartmentalise things and troubleshoot before really getting to the bottom of the problem."

One year into the project, we implemented a customised leadership programme focused on "learning on the job". The principles behind this programme were ambitious: it should be cross border, cross functional and cross cultural. We developed the architecture and design of this one-year programme in collaboration with internal and external colleagues. It involved four learning groups (of 10–15 people each) meeting simultaneously at the same location on four occasions (for a three-day module) and also working outside these modules on projects designed to create sustainable change in the organisation. This programme seemed almost doomed to fail in the first module, when participants complained, "There are too many elements of self-organisation involved, it's too interactive, we aren't learning enough from the external experts." The internal project manager for the leadership programme – a board member – remained unswerving, a pillar of strength in the face of this opposition. Without his strength, the doubts voiced by all the participants would certainly have led to the programme being stopped. He embodied the opinion: "Let's really try to change something. Let's start thinking about the good of the company instead of just protecting our own interests."

We coached the organizing committee for the manager conference, and they completely redesigned this annual meeting of over 500 international managers, turning it into an interactive, workshop-based, communication and experience-oriented event. Issues that "touched nerves" across the company were now discussed openly at this conference and looked at in a new light and with new insight. Customers and other stakeholders (e.g. the works council) were integrated in the programme and more attention paid to their opinions. This event now reflected the economic and emotional situation in the company as a whole. Every one of the managers saw themselves – this was apparent in the workshops – as part of the system and recognised the contribution they could make to improving the situation.

The company-wide planning process was also restructured, although not until after almost 18 months of consulting and coaching. The six divisional heads no longer felt responsible simply for their own divisions, but also for those of their colleagues. Feedback processes became the norm. "Getting involved in the affairs" of another division was no longer seen as a threat, but as a gesture of support and a willingness to share responsibility. Of course, there were also differences of opinion and "emotional conflicts", but these altercations had a positive effect: better quality in planning and thus more precise predictions, bringing greater credibility both internally and with the banks.

The members of the core group gradually stopped complaining that they didn't have enough time to meet so often. "I've learned that you need to slow down before you can speed up. Without these time-outs, we would never have got to the crux of our problems so quickly."

Again and again, we steered the core group to the limits of their hierarchical responsibilities, prior conceptions and experience. In the process, previously linear ways of thinking developed almost naturally into a new "networked" way of thinking, i.e. the acceptance of the need to include the overall context and processes in deliberations. Their ability to deal with uncertainty and complexity grew. The groups became the "hyper-experts in complexity management", providing the necessary backup to their individual members. "Mental development" was achieved through reflection and feedback processes. We never gave up asking questions addressed at the meta level: "How do you explain the use of these decision-making processes? Do you recognise any patterns? If so, what are they? Why do you think appropriate steps have not been taken? Where are the collective barriers? What is the good in the bad? What is your contribution?"

The willingness to provide and accept feedback continued to grow – both at an individual and a corporate level. Inviting guests to core group meetings to discuss important issues in person became almost a matter of course: plant managers came to talk about error sources, customers to discuss requirements or voice criticism and suppliers to examine business relationships.

Similar invitations were extended to the regional large group events, to meetings between units and in the establishment of customer parliaments. We constructed the frame, but it was the core group that organised itself and the processes. Of course, one year down the line, everyone knew what was meant by "steering the context" or "self-organisation" – and it was at this stage that we provided verbal and written input on the corresponding theories and models. Regular project evaluations increased the willingness to continue with the development processes. We asked the various target groups to give us their opinions on the change process, reflected on its company-wide image and then decided what the subsequent activities should be. Only later did we give this procedure a name: "systemic process loop".

The principle of "learning and self-governance through reflection" became practical reality. In some divisions, regular team development meetings were held that began with everyone stating what "really touched a nerve with them". They were followed by joint hypothesis-building sessions, not to collect facts, but to create a shared image of the overall situation and establish relationships between people, departments, content and stakeholders. A new process-oriented way of perceiving things, processing information and thinking emerged. Providing mutual feedback and negotiating expectations became far more a matter of course.

Employee appraisals also became an established part of company life, and we developed recommendations for this process with the core group. People found it less difficult to recognise their own contributions. They realised the issue was not one of tools and techniques; it was a question of attitudes and mindsets.

We are aware we have dived almost headlong into the main activities of the core group in the above description of the "Chance" project and we did so with good reason: time and again we find ourselves fascinated by the results that can be achieved using relatively unspectacular means and methods. But we would now like to return to the start.

We firmly believe that the system diagnosis at the start of a project lays the foundations for a "new way of thinking" and would therefore like to take a closer look at this fundamental initial step using the "Chance" project as an example.

To create for ourselves an overall picture of the whole company, we (the external consultants) had to assimilate not only the hard facts but also the corporate culture, i.e. the way people think, make decisions and act in the company. In other words, the way the company "breathes". We carried out 30 two-hour group interviews – with eight people to a group – across the company. The members of the core group suggested that they should also conduct interviews in order to obtain their own impressions of the situation at the company's key international sites. We agreed to this somewhat unusual request.

The core group members received a crash course in interview techniques, accompanied us to the interviews and subsequently helped us to interpret the results using the "sequence analysis method" (cf. Froschauer and Lueger 2003). We began by analyzing the manifest results, then searched for the information "between the lines", construed the latent issues and interpreted the subtle signals. Where did people face problems? What subjects were taboo? How did the group members interact during the interviews? How did they treat us? What conclusions could be drawn about the latent patterns and cultural elements of the system?

Although the method met with some initial criticism ("It's like trying to read tea leaves!"), a new sensitivity for the finer tones, undertones, hidden meaning and symbolism in what had been communicated developed during the interpretation process as the core group became more sensitive to such issues. The images that were revealed became more sophisticated and complex, yet sometimes also more oppressive. Discussing these images created and reinforced awareness, relieved pressure, motivated the group and generated learning processes, thereby creating a new reality.

The core group gradually stopped making linear assumptions ("Management is to blame!"). They recognised not only that "it takes two to tango", but also that "everyone has to assume responsibility for their own situation and not see themselves simply as victims of circumstance". They learned not to reject differences, but to see variety as "the spice of life". They accepted that one-sided solutions are pointless and almost always spell disaster. "Simply doing more of the same would be like wasting time on a lost cause. We have to learn to adopt a new perhaps more relaxed and involved attitude to our tasks and problems."

The expectations encountered in these interviews ignited such pressure for action in the core group that these visits became an annual event in the organisational development process. Even top management seized upon them as an ideal source of feedback. They became known as "mission road shows" and were used as forums for discussing those issues that "affected" people most. As time went on, this process helped increase trust in top management across the entire company.

Summary

One central effect of this process was the news that corporate earnings had improved. The company's market value increased, and optimism about the future grew. The "emotional turnaround" had been achieved: "This company is once again a fun, satisfying place to work." The learning process is still ongoing, but has now become a permanent development process "managed" by the staff themselves. We only provide support in a supervisory capacity.

Consulting projects of this kind are always great adventures, since there is always a risk that they might ultimately fail. It takes a great deal of energy on our part to assume a different role to the one expected of us. We don't provide the solutions. Instead, it's the employees who are the experts. As process experts, we do not simply serve up the longed-for recipes for success, we guide the system towards its goals using carefully chosen interventions to activate new processes of awareness. In addition to the satisfying and positive aspects of this work, it also brings to light the dark side of systems and people. This awakens fears, painful emotions, conflicts and ambivalences – all of which need to be addressed and dealt with.

The following description by the chairman of the board presents a very graphic image of how adventurous an organisational development journey can be for clients:

"I initially took a very rational approach to this project. All the other change programmes we had tried with conventional consultants had lead nowhere. When I heard about this approach, I thought: 'Oh well, if there is nothing else for it, let's give it a try.' I had no idea where we were going. The territory we now find ourselves in was completely new to us. We were guided here gently by Königswieser & Network. I felt a bit like Christopher Columbus. He set sail for the Old World, for the familiar shores of the West Indies, and landed instead in unfamiliar America to discover the New World. This journey into new, uncharted territory was – and is – a real adventure. If I had known back then what we were letting ourselves in for, I would not have had the courage to set sail on this course in the first place. But with what I know now, I can say one thing with certainty: 'We should have started out on this journey sooner.' We now know so much more about ourselves and our real problems. Before embarking on this kind of change process, we were like a ship that continually ran aground in shallow waters on the rocks we had not seen ahead. Like icebergs, all we saw were those parts above the water. Now we have developed a radar system of our own and can move forward, full steam ahead. It will be very interesting to see where we go from here."

When we look back at this case study from the professional meta level, we see that a range of different interventions were used. We also clearly see how interwoven these interventions are at the architecture, design and tools levels, and how difficult and time-consuming the process of stimulating complex systems can be.

In the following chapters, we will take a more detailed look at the "Chance" project, our methods and the interventions described above.

2. What is Systemic Consulting?

To introduce the reader to systemic consulting, we have deliberately chosen to use a concrete example of our own consulting activities to best demonstrate where the intricacies of this approach lie.

Our aim with this introduction is to present our approach and ideas in a practical, demonstrative and comprehensible manner. Nevertheless, or perhaps even for this reason, the terms used have to be carefully selected and clearly defined to make complicated issues easier to *understand* while at the same time avoiding simplification. Einstein once said, "Everything should be made as simple as possible, but not simpler than it is." We have tried to do justice to this dictum.

Thoughts that have been put down on paper like this text are made up of sentences, words and recurring key terms. Terms represent basic trains of thought; they are theory in condensed form. That is why we have chosen to begin with a discussion of the key terms "systemic" and "consulting". These are closely linked to two other terms, "organisation" and "development". Our understanding of these four terms, the connections between them and what they can be used to explain, builds on a long tradition of attempts to describe and understand the phenomena that are peculiar to "organisms" and which differentiate them from trivial machines.

We will then take a look at the origins and roots of the systemic approach and the resultant understanding of organisations.

2.1 The Systemic View – Definitions

By *consulting* we mean quite generally that a person, group, organisation or company receives advice from someone else to do (or not do) one thing or the other. People generally ask for "advice" when they are uncertain of how to proceed in a particular situation, and it is in such situations of uncertainty and their accompanying insecurity that they usually seek the advice of consultants.

The advice of an expert can help to directly resolve a problematic[3] situation if the advisor either already knows the solution to the problem or can help those seeking advice to find the right solution. This is known as "helping people to help themselves" and is aptly reflected in the saying: "Give a man a fish and he will eat for a day. Teach a man to fish and he will eat for a lifetime."

Systemic consulting aims to initiate, guide and support long-term, sustainable processes of learning and renewal with the goal of making systems (organisations) better able to survive, prosper and increase their efficiency. This lies at the heart of the systemic approach.

We use the term "systemic consulting" to refer to a very particular approach to the consulting process. "Systemic consultants" base their actions on the so-called "systemic attitude", assume a "systemic view" of situations and a "systemic understanding" of individuals, groups, organisations and processes[4].

But what does seeing an individual, a group or a company as a living "system" – and "treating" them accordingly – actually mean? What is a system? What are the consequences of seeing companies in this way? What is a systemic view? To answer these questions properly, we must first review the cornerstones of systems theory.

A prerequisite for understanding "systems theory" – as with all other theories and views of the world – is to see the theory itself as an attempt to explain something, as a "*thesis*". Theses are assumptions regarding what we consider to be real or the notion that in particular circumstances and under particular conditions something specific will or will not happen if a particular thing is or is not done. In other words, they are attempts to explain the links between actions and their effects. This is how, for example, we have learned to understand the dramatic effects even the smallest bit of interference, such as the wiping out of a link in the food chain, can have on the ecosystem: "everything is connected to everything else". Through this "deeper insight" into the complex relationships between causes and their effects, we also come to understand what an "ecosystem" is and how it functions. We refer to this as the "hanging mobile effect", because virtually every intervention in a system ultimately has an effect on the entire system.

Our attempts at explanation, our theories and our theses are, however, also part of what happens in the system, because as humans we form part of the system "society", "world" or "nature". No matter where we look, we always see ourselves, our own mental constructions and projections.

Figure 1: The View of the World as a Subjective Construct

Systems theory is therefore a "view of the world", a wilful, idiosyncratic attempt at explanation, which always refers back to itself in the explanation. We call this form of self-reference "reflexivity".

This characterisation is, however, difficult for humans to accept, since we are used to seeing our knowledge of the world as objective, as a truth that exists independently of mankind.

2.2 Origins of the Systemic View of the World – Roots of Systems Theory

The term "system" comes from the Greek and means literally "*to stand + together*". It refers to a whole that exists only through the working together of its parts, or as Aristotle said, "The whole is more than the sum of its parts." But although this is an age-old concept for describing particular phenomena, it was not until the beginning of the 20th century that a general, all encompassing "theory of systems" actually began to develop. Significantly, the starting points for the new systems theory lay in the fields of biology and physics, where scientists found themselves unable to make further progress using traditional, mechanistic models.

We were surprised to discover it had primarily been scientists and scholars working in Vienna, Graz and Prague around 1900 who concerned themselves with the question of how to explain the emergence of order and disorder in systems (thermodynamics – law of entropy). They found themselves facing the problem that the traditional conceptual images of classical physics – *made up of rigid, fixed elements = object* plus *cause/force/action* leads to *effect/ motion/reaction* – could not be used to describe states of order or disorder and then explain their transitions, emergence and passage. They needed a new scientific language with different conceptual images and paradigms: in short, a new theory.

Of key importance for the development of systems theory was the fact that the scholars working on this "project" not only assumed an interdisciplinary approach, they were without exception all universal scholars (natural scientists, mathematicians and philosophers) researching all manner of different disciplines. Of course, at that time, there was no talk of "systems theory"; discussions focused on questions of philosophy, epistemology, linguistics, natural sciences, economics, politics and art (cf. Janik and Toulmin 1973).

In the so-called "Vienna Circle", whose members included Rudolf Carnap, Kurt Gödel, Hans Hahn and Moritz Schlick (cf. Geier 1995), scientists were encouraged by advances in physics (Albert Einstein, Niels Bohr) and initially tried to build on the work of Ernst Mach and Ludwig Boltzmann to develop a theory of theories, a general theory of scientific knowledge that adhered to strict mathematical logic, under the title "The Scientific View of the World"[5] (scientific theory: Gottlob Frege, Bertrand Russell, Ludwig Wittgenstein).

The conceptual images used to explain system changes and the *system/environment difference*[6] (e.g. living, growing, dying) did not, however, fit with this new theory. Some of these systemic concepts and key terms date as far back as Aristotle, Goethe and Darwin. But it was not until later that they were taken seriously by Ernst Mach (1838–1916, Vienna-Graz-Prague), Christian von Ehrenfels (1859–1932, Vienna-Graz-Prague), Max Wertheimer (1880–1943, Prague-Vienna-USA), Ludwig von Bertalanffy (1901–1972, Vienna-Prague-USA), Heinz von Foerster (1911-2002, Vienna-Breslau-USA) and Ernst von Glasersfeld (*1917, Vienna-Zurich-USA) as possible instruments of scientific knowledge and became established systemic key terms[7]. The most important of these are listed below in Fig. 2.

- Order (patterns, rules, structures) – disorder (chaos, entropy)
- Transition (development, change, history, genesis) from chaos to order to chaos
- Permanence (durability, rigidity, unchangeableness) – changeability (change, dynamics, evolution)
- Delimitation (unity, internal, self-referencing) – communication (openness, exchange, external, environment)
- Information (formation, establishment of order, provision of instruction) – deformation (destruction, elimination, downfall)
- Complexity (multiple layers, relationships, meanings) – simplicity (unity, identity, unambiguity)
- Difference (deviation, distinction, suspense between system/environment) – balance (leveling out)

Figure 2: Systemic Key Terms

Constructing a solid theory out of these building blocks, a theory that can stand without the use of metaphors and pictorial comparisons, is no easy task. This is illustrated by the fact that scientists are still working today on the formulation of a unified theory, with many remaining sceptical because such a theory seems to contain nothing they can "make tangible".

The biologist and philosopher von Bertalanffy was the first to piece the elements together into a "general systems theory" (1928/1936/1976). The systems approach was developed further between 1930 and 1960 in the USA, primarily by the Austrian emigrants working in close collaboration with their colleagues and followers. The biological application of systems theory was augmented increasingly by applications from the fields of social sciences, psychology and information theory (informatics). It was not until around 1950 that scientists in Europe began to focus on systemic explanatory models once again.

Fig. 3 illustrates the development of systems theory and the links between the different theoretical approaches.

One of the fascinating aspects about the development of (open)[8] systems theory is that its original aspirations to adequately describe reality using exact mathematical logic (neopositivism) almost resulted in the opposite effect: our knowledge of the world is made up of constructions that are not "unreal" in the sense of illusions and fiction, but actively create a reality that makes "sense" to us. Understanding and developing theories is a system activity of human society. It creates an image of itself and the world for society. There is no such thing as an

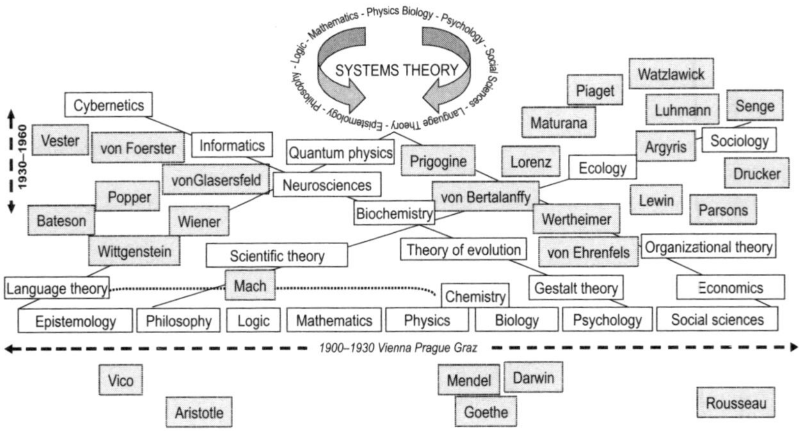

Figure 3: Development of Systems Theory

objective, independent observer. This is the position taken by radical *constructivism* (cf. von Foerster/Pörksen 2001).

This leads to another interesting phenomenon: if we think the systems model through to completion as Niklas Luhmann, Heinz von Foerster, Humberto Maturana and Francisco Varela did, we uncover a strange paradox.[9] On the one hand, systems theory requires that all systems are themselves made up of systems and these, in turn, of subsystems, each with their own differences, dependencies, activities and functional relationships, i.e. that the whole cosmos is a system of systems. For this reason, systems theory has to raise claims to being a "universal theory", similar to religious images of the world. On the other hand, however, systems theory has to see itself as an activity, a function of a specific system, which would mean that its claim to meaning can only be validated within this actual system. How other systems "see" themselves and their environment is a completely different matter. This corresponds to the position taken by *relativism*.

When we and a group of colleagues and friends first began applying systemic concepts to organisational consulting, we found this paradox particularly difficult to come to terms with: How do you combine the universalist, absolutist claims of systems theory with an attitude of modest "relativisation"? (cf. Königswieser and Lutz 1992.)

Descriptive and explanatory models based on systems theory are used to consider cases that involve complex interactions, reciprocal effects and dynamic developments. Researchers emphasise different aspects of the systems concept, depending on their individual field of study.

We will now describe some of the aspects we consider to be of particular relevance, thereby illustrating that systems theory offers a less unified and closed view of the world than a mechanistic view. As is the case for other disciplines – such as economics or psychology – there are also different trends and schools of thought in the systems approach, depending on what it is being applied to and the elements of the systems concept being emphasised.

For example, the *biological understanding of systems* considers in particular the "principle of self-organisation in living systems" (homeostasis = self-organisation; autopoiesis = self-producing, self-maintaining), but is also applied to knowledge processes by authors such as Maturana and Varela (1987), Gregory Bateson (2000) and Frederic Vester (1983). Chemists like Ilya Prigogine (cf. Prigogine and Stengers 1984) and physicists like Fritjof Capra (2000) also try to reinterpret the development of order in their fields of research using a systemic view of the world.

Social scientists concern themselves primarily with "communication" within and between systems by means of special "codes". For example, Luhmann (1984) or Bernhard Giesen (1991) described "fully differentiated functional systems" within society under the aspects of "operative difference" between system/environment and "communication" (codification) as follows: everything is communication.

For scientists studying questions of the *steerability/controllability of complex systems* (cybernetics = the science of communication and steering/control) such as von Foerster (1984), the answer lies in what is known as "reflexive self-reference". As soon as someone begins to observe, understand and intervene in a system, they become part of a process in that system. Continuous loops of interaction and reciprocal effect are initiated between the controlling system and the system being controlled, which can only be deciphered by observing the observing (cybernetics of cybernetics = second order cybernetics = controlling the controlling = steering the context).

A similar loop concept is used by *communication theorists* and *epistemologists* such as Bateson (1995) and Paul Watzlawick (Watzlawick *et al.* 2000) and *cognitive psychologists* like Jean Piaget (1992). Consider the following situation: when people do something with the intention of achieving something else (because they consider it important or sensible), they will either succeed and reach their goal, or they will fail. If they do not reach their goal, they will usually change their approach, their strategy. Feedback helps them learn to take more appropriate actions. However, they could also reflect on themselves, their goals, desires, standards and values and come to the conclusion that there is a discrepancy in the relationship between "starting point of action – strategy/technique – goal of action". This reflection would involve learning how to improve the original learning. *Double loop learning* means learning to learn; it enables people to reshape patterns of thinking and has a self-regulating effect.

The search for suitable interventions for complex systems also plays an important role in systemic *family therapy*. Difficult family situations cannot usually be resolved through individual therapy: they require an understanding of the living conditions, life histories and interaction of everyone involved. Problems are seen as symptoms. In the Milan approach to family therapy based on the work of Mara Selvini Palazzoli (Selvini Palazzoli et al. 1978), a number of effective systemic intervention methods have been developed (paradox interventions, reframing, circular questions) that can be used to help reshape established problem patterns (or "rigid loops").

Finally, all these different approaches eventually come together in *organisational* and *management theories*, which consider not only individuals, group dynamics, learning and control, but also general issues in society and economics (environment) or technology (infrastructure, informatics). A number of systemic models have been developed, e.g. by Peter Senge (1996), Chris Argyris (Argyris and Schön 1978), Bo Hedberg (1981) and Helmut Willke (2000), each focusing on different aspects. Similarly, our own systemic approach to consulting draws on a number of different concepts (cf. Königswieser and Lutz 1992).

All these individual varieties of the systemic approach have a number of things in common. The systemic paradigm or model of thinking moves away from the mechanistic or mechanical model, the belief in objectivity: it applies the principle of multiple perspectives and puts the emphasis on self-governance. It addresses the complexity and dynamics of lived worlds (*Lebenswelten*) and their associated uncertainty and uncontrollability.

The key differences between these two paradigms are summarised in Fig. 4.

Mechanistic View of the World	Systemic View of the World
Objectivity, one truth, fixed laws	Construction of reality, many "truths", theses
Right-wrong, guilty-innocent	Context dependent, usefulness, connectivity
(External) control	Self-control, self-organisation
Linear cause-and-effect chains	Multiple interaction and reciprocal effect, feedback loops
Measurable, fixed difference	Differentiating oneself, changing
Linear progression, changing	Development, changing and maintaining, unblocking
Formal logic, no contradiction, exclusion	Integration of conflicting views, involvement
Hard facts, rational relationships	Integration of hard and soft factors (emotions, intuitions, communication processes)
Roles: doers, leaders and the lead, manipulation	Roles: motivators, gardeners, enablers, development guide, coach
Methods: instruction, orders, commands, learning by trial and error	Methods: listening, asking questions, dialogue, discussion, reflection, learning to learn

Figure 4: Mechanistic and Systemic Views of the World

2.3 The Systemic Understanding of Organisations

2.3.1 What is an Organisation?

To be able to intervene in organisations, you must first equip yourself with an adequate "theory" of what constitutes an organisation. However, answering the question "What is an organisation?" proves a more difficult endeavour than might initially be expected (cf. Weick 1985, p. 41-94). In everyday use, we seem to know exactly what we mean by the word "organisation" and use it to refer to very definite entities like public and family-owned companies, the police, religious charities, Greenpeace, the United Nations or the Mafia. Although this label presumes some form of commonality and comparability, it does not provide an understanding and perception of what an organisation is and how it works.

Can you actually see and observe an organisation? Do you enter an organisation when you go through the door or sign a contract of employment? What happens when the staff go home for the weekend? Where is the organisation then? Do the employees take the organisation home with them in their heads or does it remain in the buildings, documents and structures left on site? Then there is another question to be asked: What does an oil company have in common with a political party, a football team or the Red Cross?

The question of commonality, of what typifies an organisation, of how organisations work or should ideally work, gains particular relevance and importance when the answers are to be used as guidelines for action and behaviour, i.e. affect the interests of those involved.

If a company owner sees his company primarily as a means of increasing his return on investment, he is more likely to think of and treat his employees accordingly. He could, theoretically, install a fully automated factory with no need for people to fulfil the same purpose. If he does so, whilst he might not have his own (human) organisation, his money-making machine will, nonetheless, still not function entirely without the need for an organisation. After all, someone has to build the factory, maintain the equipment, sell and – above all – buy its products. This means, however, that the label "organisation" cannot be limited just to "the company" in the narrow sense of the word.

An organisation, therefore, is a multi-dimensional "social system" with its own inner world that really only exists (and can only exist) through being a sub-system of larger systems or communicating and establishing relationships with other systems.

All organisations have one thing in common: they outlast the moment, the current action and interaction, the change. In this respect they are similar to organisms, which exist for a given lifetime, grow, develop and then die. Seen in this way, organisations exist in the "*suspense*" between permanence and transience. This would be the *vitalistic view* of organisation.

If you ask a company employee, a firefighter or a consultant what they do in the organisation, why they work with other people, the answer will probably start with "because". The reasons can be manifold, but they always follow the same logic: I want to achieve something specific through my action, e.g. earn money and be needed (rationality of action/ intention). If the goals of an action seem attainable, doing something makes "sense". Seen from this perspective, the organisation is a necessary partnership of convenience. This would be the *voluntaristic-interactionistic view* of organisation.

When looked at from the interests, needs and desires of its members, an organisation is a union with a rational goal. To reach this goal (e.g. mutual prosperity) through cooperation, to ensure the continuation of the interaction, to prevent the union collapsing and suppress conflicts of interest and power struggles, agreements are reached, membership defined, rules introduced, contracts signed, roles and functions distributed, work processes established and infrastructures and sanctions put in place. "Sensible" structures create order in the organisation. This would be the *rationalistic-structuralistic view* of organisation.

This might apply to a football club, but certainly not to the armed forces or even a village community. In government agencies, local authorities and institutions, i.e. in bureaucratic organisations, the members of the organisation do not make the rules and establish the structures. They are replaceable and have to comply. It is the structured whole that determines what will be done, while the internal order is enforced from outside, e.g. by the "governmental apparatus" (structural determinism).

Conversely, in a village community things often take place without planning or particular intent. Sometimes they happen in a more traditional manner, sometimes chaotically or by chance. Some things are the result of good fortune, others of catastrophe. Depending on the circumstances, the village community organises itself and develops more or less haphazardly, just as a plant blossoms in good soil and withers in poor. This is referred to as "emergent self-organisation" or the *naturalistic view* of organisation.

Traditional business- and economics-oriented organisational theory sees organisations as target-oriented, intentional and rationally constructed entities in which people's actions always have a purpose. Systemic organisational theory shatters this image by emphasizing complexity and dynamics, ambivalence and contradiction, processes and conflicts as characteristics of organisations (cf. Weick 1985).

2.3.2 What Does a "Systemic View" of Organisations Mean?

How exactly does the "systemic view" of organisations differ from traditional views?

As for other applications of the systemic approach, *complexity and dynamics* as characteristics of living systems play a fundamental role in the systemic view of organisations. By complexity we mean the non-linear, non-mechanistic, non-one-dimensional connection between what happens on the inside and what happens on the outside.

The actors in these systems are people with different needs, desires, fears, traits, likes, dislikes, abilities, limitations, memories and visions. People are by no means trivial machines – they are incredibly complex. They are not simply members of a particular organisation, e.g. employees of a company, they also live their private and public lives as members of different communities in which they play a role and which, in turn, influence them. All these aspects contribute to each and every communication situation. In addition to this complexity in inter-human relationships, people also have to deal with the many and varied demands of the real world: using tools, operating machines, dealing with time and resources, and mastering production and information processes.

To deal with this complexity, people build themselves *patterns* of action, behaviour and thinking they can repeat: habits, rituals, stereotypical behaviour, expectations, prejudices, sense constructs and views of the world. These patterns reduce complexity to a more acceptable, manageable level. They make events seem expectable, even predictable, and are ideally continuously adapted and reshaped to meet the requirements of the current situation.

This means that the inner world of an organisation is controlled through *reduction in complexity* and that the organisation controls itself through shared meanings, value hierarchies and visions, through conventions, rituals and customs, through role allocation and hierarchies and, above all, through the objectification of agreements.

The objectification of consensus and difference is achieved both by building artificial structures (infrastructure, laws, walls, fences, etc.) and through internalisation (habits, perception and expectation patterns, behaviour, prejudices, etc). These are then used to continually differentiate between alternatives (e.g. important – unimportant, relevant –irrelevant, useful – useless, permitted – forbidden, desirable – undesirable, applicable – inapplicable, etc.). Differentiating in this way involves carrying out selections and is referred to in systems theory as "*information*". As Bateson (1972) said, "Information is a difference which makes a difference."

When we talk in everyday terms about "exchanging information and knowledge", we are referring to a flow of information between individuals or organisations. Yet from a systemic point of view this is not possible. Why?

Let's take a look at the argument that the information process can only take place within a system and never between a system and its environment. That sounds absurd. What can it mean?

Consider two people talking to each other. Each of these two individuals is a system (an organism) and processes "information" within themselves. When two people talk to each other, they establish a new, social system (group, community, society) in which information is also processed. Each individual is therefore a subsystem of this (new) system. What goes on in each partner's "head and mind" is something totally different to what happens between them. The speaker transmits noises or sends visual signals which are capable of penetrating the borders of the listener's system, i.e. his senses (eyes and ears). The listener has to recognise what he hears as a code (as a "symbol" or sign for something it is not), decode these signals and translate them into "information" in his own cognitive psychological system. To be able to do so, he has to have internalised the structure of the social system, its codes and their purpose. In other words, he has to know its language and its "language games" (*Sprachspiele*). We refer to this as "structural coupling". He has to carry the order structures of the social system with him in order to be able to connect to it, communicate and understand.

In other words, no information can – strictly speaking – pass across system borders. In the above example, what goes on in the heads of the two partners in conversation is an information process in their psychological/mental system, and what takes place between them is a social process. Neither process can be compared directly with the other. Each input and output across system borders must first run through a *transformation process* before it can set off an "information process" within its own or another system. This also fits with the claim of systems theorists that it is not really possible to see into the darkness and understand the inner workings of a system. It is a black box.

Therefore, an organisation builds itself internal *order structures* not simply to maintain its inner world, but also to enable it to assert itself in its environment or to develop *the capability to connect to and carry out information processes with* other systems (cf. Baecker 1999).

The problems an organisation encounters in developing its ability to interact with other systems lie primarily in its hardened internal (reified and internalised) order structures, which obstruct or prevent its ability to learn, adapt and react to a dynamic environment. The concept of the "learning organisation" (cf. Senge 1996) pushes systems thinking to centre stage. Systems thinking as "fifth discipline" represents the basic principle behind "the management of organisational learning processes": a "learning organisation" learns and is capable of developing and learning.

Since organisations exist in a continuous suspense between permanence (internal reduction in complexity) and change (learning, growth) and tension between their inner world and environment, they develop "history" as the continuum of experiences of the past, perceptions of the present and expectations of the future (cf. Ortner 2003a). Each social system develops its own history – its own view of itself and the world – which, in light of the above, is only meaningful to insiders, i.e. the members of that system.

2.3.3 What Does the Systemic View of Organisations Mean for Consulting?

Our understanding of consulting as the "systemic organisational development" described in this book has evolved over many years. It draws in particular on the models developed by those scholars with whom we have discussed our work and with whom we have developed close relationships and, in some cases, even friendships over the years. These include Niklas Luhmann, Fritjof Capra and the systemic family therapist Sigi Hirsch from the Milan school. Psychoanalytical and group dynamics concepts also play an important role in our work, not only because they form part of our own background and qualifications, but also because they open up new, additional perspectives. Issues such as the "collective unconscious" in large groups, defence mechanisms or deep-seated "archaic" emotions and conflicts all play important roles in a change process.

Fig. 5 illustrates the influence of the various knowledge domains on our approach.

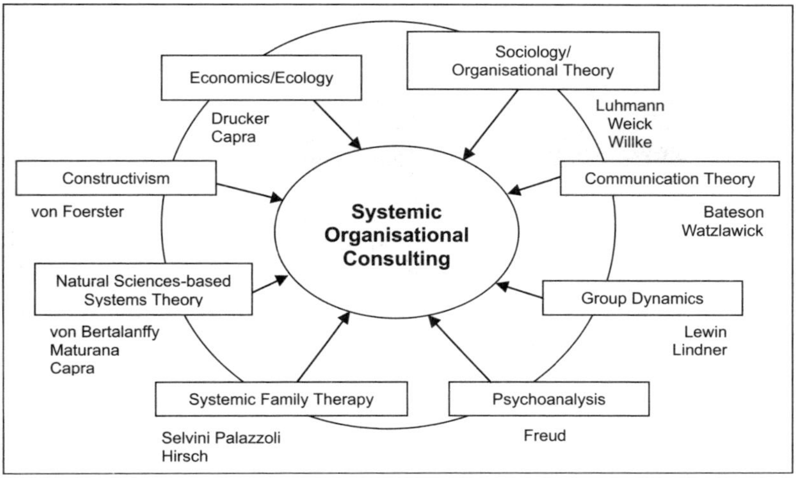

Figure 5: Fields of Influence on our Understanding of Systemic Organisational Consulting

To summarise, the following list emphasises the basic assumptions that are of particular significance in the planned use of systemic consulting interventions:

- Organisations do not function like trivial machines. They do not simply work at the push of a button and can therefore neither be controlled directly nor completely understood.
- They constantly reproduce themselves through communication, are in a state of permanent change and continually create new order structures in the form of retained stories, recorded successes and agreed perception patterns and expectations.
- This "self-image" gains intensity in the sense constructs and views of the world projected as models from inside the system to the environment. Internal order structures, sense constructs and images of the world create security and stability within the organisation, yet at the same time obstruct its ability to react to changes in a dynamic, rapidly changing environment.
- Organisations can learn from their environment not only in times of crisis and pressure, but also proactively by assuming an active and creative role in reshaping themselves and their respective environments.

With the above information and background in mind, we will now take a closer look at "systemic consulting" in the narrower sense of the term.

2.4 Developing the Consultant-Client System

A consulting relationship involves interaction and communication between two social systems: the organisation seeking consulting services as *client system* (CLS) and the organisation providing the consulting services as *consultant system* (COS). The interaction between the CLS and the COS for the duration of the consulting project results in the establishment of a third system, the *consultant-client system* (CCS):

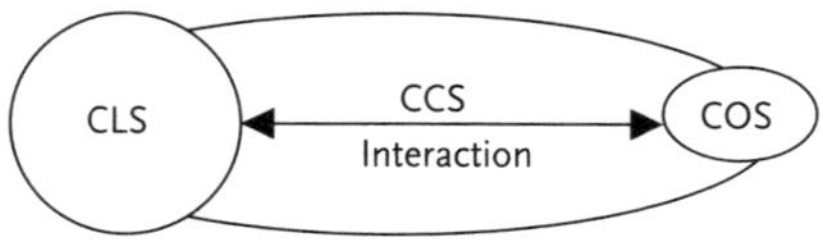

Figure 6: Consultant-Client System

Both the client system and the consultant system delimit themselves as organisations from their environment, yet at the same time also communicate with it (dynamic system-environment difference). The COS represents a (potential) environment for the CLS and vice versa. It is only by signing a *consulting agreement* that both systems declare the other a relevant environment. The consultants can now take up their roles and begin to meet expectations.

An *intervention* is a targeted communication between the two systems designed to achieve a specific effect within the CLS, whereby the CLS is assumed to be autonomous.

As far as the COS is concerned, the members of the CLS are the real experts on their own activities, and cannot therefore simply be "taught" to do things differently. The COS provides process know-how, further context-related subject know-how and, above all, the important external view on an internal situation.

According to our definition, systemic consulting can be summarised by the following principles:

- *Limitations:* An intervention is only an attempt to motivate the CLS to do something. It is up to the CLS to do what it can with this intervention. The possibilities for exerting external influence on what happens in the system are limited.

- *Balance between changing and maintaining:* The COS can only point to and illustrate the tension between changing and maintaining, highlight any contradictions and open up these issues to be addressed. The CLS alone decides what to do with this information.
- *Hanging mobile effect*: Start where the energy is already to be found. As with a hanging mobile, an intervention in one area will also have an effect on others.
- *Integration*: Do not separate hard factors from soft. The "SIM model" (Systemic Integration Model; cf. Königswieser et al. 2001, p. 53) illustrates the reciprocal effects between vision, strategy, structure and culture.
- *Bespoke, process-oriented procedure*: Connective interventions must be planned in context and continually adapted throughout the process.
- *Reflection:* To do justice to its role and task, the COS must continually run through reflection loops (see Figure 11).
- *Connective ability:* Consultants are second order observers (unlike employees of the company, who are first order observers) and must therefore try to identify the structures and system logic behind the actors and intervene in a relevant and connective manner.
- *Partnership:* The COS must itself be a stable system, establish clear rules regarding proximity/distance to the client and become surplus to requirements.
- *Principle of multiple perspectives*: Looking at things from different perspectives and from the standpoints of different, conflicting factions.
- *Implementation focus:* Implementation is an integral element in the process right from the start.

The experiences of both the CLS and the COS in dealing with their environments are reflected in the development of the CCS. Consequently, the COS will usually be seen and treated by the CLS in the way it has learned to act in its relationships with the relevant systems in its environment, e.g. either with mistrust, lack of commitment and lack of respect, or with trust, commitment, respect and high regard. Commercial companies tend to have more cost-benefit-oriented expectations of the CCS, while non-profit organisations are inclined to place more emphasis on values, ethical or political criteria. Two other factors that play a role are the amount of strain the situation places on the CLS and the profile of the COS.

One phenomenon that can be put to good use in consulting work is the "resonance phenomenon" (cf. Elkaim 1990). Just as physical bodies react to certain frequencies, living systems transfer resonance (e.g. stress and moods) to each other. Patterns and conflicts observed, for example, in the CLS also appear in the COS. When used for reflection, they are an important source of information about the CLS.

3. The Basic Principles of Our Approach

This chapter takes a more detailed look at some of the fundamental principles behind systemic consulting.

3.1 Attitude

No matter how sophisticated the theories or how well thought out the techniques, they will all be to no avail if the consultant doesn't have the "right" *attitude* or *mindset*. We believe that developing such an attitude is fundamental to a systemic approach to organisational development. Attitude lies at the core of systemic work and is the thread that runs through all our training programmes.

The term "attitude" is closely linked to identity, character, mindset, perception and constructions of reality. It refers not only to the way we carry ourselves and the manner in which we act, but also to our state of mind or our feelings. We talk, for example, about people having a positive (or negative) attitude to work.

Attitude affects the way we both think and behave. It is the basis, yet at the same time also the product, of our thoughts and behaviour. It is formed by our history, mental models, experiences and validations and, in turn, influences our view of the world.

Attitude is reflected in the way we relate to ourselves and our environment, the way we deal with our internal and external worlds, the way we conduct our relationships and the way we think and perceive. It reflects what we perceive to be true or false.

Our attitude also has consequences for our self-image, our view of what constitutes professionalism and our preferred concepts and methods.

So how would we describe the systemic attitude? What makes it instantly recognizable? The following statements illustrate the characteristics of a systemic attitude:

- "There is no objectivity; I have to take a closer look at the context. Everything a person does gains meaning if I know the context. It is about making room for more than one perspective ("principle of multiple perspectives"). To orient myself, I have to build hypotheses because my own observations are always subjective and only a part of the whole."

- "Conflicting opinions are part of life. Differences bring richness and variety. What's important is the balance, the emphasis on things that have been pushed to one side. Such issues often represent the dark side of a problem. Conflicts might hurt, but they also provide opportunity for development. Resistance is energy that needs to be used."
- "Things are the way they are. We must first understand the purpose and meaning behind typical patterns in the system. The right attitude helps to lessen the drama, identify the good in the bad (when the system focus is on deficits) or the bad in the good (when the system tends towards idealisation)."

The following story helps illustrate this point.

An old man and his son together worked a small family farm. They had only one horse to pull the plough. One day, the horse ran away. "How awful," said the neighbours, "what bad luck." "Who knows," replied the old farmer, "if it is good luck or bad?" The following week, the horse returned to the farm from the mountains with five wild horses for the stable. "How wonderful," said the neighbours, "what good luck!" "Good luck or bad," said the old farmer, "who knows?" The next morning, the son was trying to tame one of the wild horses when he fell and broke his leg. "How awful! What bad luck!" – "Good luck? Bad luck?" War was declared, and the army arrived in the village to conscript all the young men. They had no use for the farmer's son with a broken leg, and so he was the only one spared. "Good luck? Bad luck?"

- "We see those apparently to blame for a problem simply as the symptom carriers. It is not about changing or analyzing individual people, but recognizing structures, relationship patterns and mindsets, and enabling people to alter their behaviour by changing the way they look at things. Everyone involved plays their own part in a problem."
- "We take a holistic approach. Everything, in principle, is contained in every unit, no matter how small, and everything is connected to everything else. A Chinese proverb says: *Each drop of water contains the secrets of a whole ocean*. No matter where we begin, what we do will ultimately always have an effect somewhere else ("hanging mobile effect")."

- "When we change the parameters of our field of vision, our perceived connections and meanings often also change. We call this 'reframing.' Consider the following example: A man and his wife, both aged 60, were walking through the woods one day, when they met a fairy. 'I will grant you one wish,' whispered the fairy to the man. Without thinking, he replied: 'I wish my wife was 20 years younger than me.' The fairy waved her magic wand and, before he knew it, the man was 80."
- "Development processes take time. Living systems have biological response times. Profound mental change does not simply happen at the push of a button."
- "We see our role in the consulting process as providers of momentum, guides on a system's journey towards developing greater problem-solving abilities. A gardener is a good example of this. He can prepare the ground, plant, cut, feed, prune and care for the plants. But he can't grow pineapples if the climate and soil won't support them. He has to know and respect the conditions that a plant needs to grow."

3.2 Relationship to the Client and to Yourself

The above characterisation of attitude also implies a certain quality in the relationship consultants have to the client and to themselves as consultants.

- "The key components of any consulting process are respect, trust in the power of self-help and a belief in the ability of people and organisations to develop."
- "We don't just work with people in positions of power, we work with people from all manner of different interest groups and hierarchy levels. We call this impartiality. We are advocates of ambivalence."
- "Since we are aware of the limitations of our intervention possibilities and take autopoiesis seriously, modesty is as much a part of our attitude as self-confidence is."
- "Feedback implies learning and self-governance. We believe in personal responsibility, in the self-healing powers of living systems, and see it as our role to activate and/or energise them. To do so, we have to know how best to put our message across."

- "Since we are trained first and foremost to see the resources and potential, rather than the deficits, we are more interested in working with opportunities, positive images of the future and options. What is going well? What are the success stories? What is the vision? This attitude opens up extended fields of action. It can help people break away from deep-seated, hardened patterns of thinking."
- "We try to find out what is blocking energy. Once these blockages have been removed, things begin to flow again. Usually the people involved themselves know best what is blocking them and what they can do to help themselves."

Embodying this attitude is not easy. You have to permanently work at yourself, distance yourself from the situation yet, at the same time, immerse yourself in it totally and use your own emotional responses as information. This is not possible without reflection and awareness, without knowing and accepting yourself, your blind spots, failings, values and limitations. Coping with uncertainty brings certainty and stability and characterises professionalism. The following story illustrates this point.

Two Zen monks, one advanced in years, the other still very young, were walking along a muddy path through the rainforest on their way home to the monastery, when they came across a beautiful woman standing helplessly at the bank of a fast flowing river. The elder monk, recognizing her dilemma, picked her up and began to carry her across the river. She smiled, wrapped her arms around his neck and held on tightly until he gently put her down on the other side. The woman bowed her head in thanks, and the two monks continued in silence on their way. Shortly before they reached the monastery gates, the young monk could contain himself no longer. "How could you take such a beautiful woman in your arms?", he cried, "Such action does not befit a monk!" The elder monk looked at his companion and replied, "I left her back there on the bank of the river. Are you still carrying her with you?"

As the thread running through all the images, values and views that characterise systemic attitude, we constantly find ourselves confronted with paradoxes and contradictions. The ability to integrate and balance out these opposite poles is what distinguishes a differentiated professional approach (see Fig. 7).

- Reflecting and learning from feedback while at the same time being spontaneous and intuitive
- Being self-confident yet modest
- Learning, experimenting, discovering, being curious and open yet at the same time respecting clear meta norms, distinctions, knowledge and position at the process level
- Being affected and getting involved but at the same time maintaining distance and composure
- Combining a sense of responsibility with a playful approach
- Giving security but also providing constructive irritation
- Including both hard facts and soft factors
- Changing yet conserving
- Slowing things down without reducing efficiency

Figure 7: Balance of Attitude Between Opposite Poles

The dimensions of attitude described above translate into orientation guidelines for the approach taken and the underlying constraints. Respecting them reduces risks and increases the possibility of success in consulting projects.

3.3 Success Factors in Systemic Consulting

Fig. 8 summarises the factors that our own experience has shown to be prerequisites for success. We use the factors listed under each of the 10 points as a form of checklist, a list of questions to help determine whether the basic requirements for the success of a project are in place or not. The questions can be answered either with a simple "yes" or "no", or rated on a scale of 0 to 10 (0 = totally disagree, 10 = totally agree). These points apply both to complex and simpler projects, e.g. those involving just one or two workshops.

Re 1: Is the contract clear? What constitutes success for the consulting project? Are the roles of the consultant, the project manager, etc. clear? Will there be an evaluation and a readjustment of the targets if something were to change?

Re 2: Were the key members of the top management team present at the initial meeting? Does the project architecture include a top management coaching element? Is there a mechanism in place for dialogue between top level management and the steering group? Does top management publicly support the project?

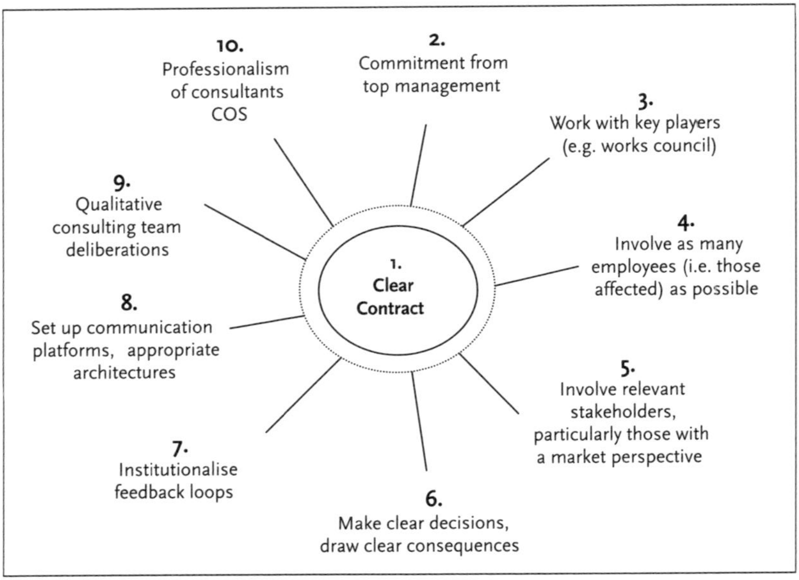

Figure 8: Success Factors and Basic Requirements

Re 3: Who are the official and unofficial key players? Is there a strong project management team? Which activities are the key players involved in? How do we cultivate our relationship with them? How many of them are members of the steering group? How many are involved in the project as a whole? Are they involved anywhere as a group?

Re 4: How are employees or sub-groups integrated into the process (interviews, projects, communication platforms)? Do the communication platforms include a good mix of hierarchical levels? How do the internal communication processes work? Is enough attention paid to suggestions from employees?

Re 5: Who or what are the most relevant stakeholders? Can they be involved? If yes, how? Have we considered the market perspective sufficiently (e.g. customers, suppliers, authorities, supervisory board)? Is there a process of co-evolution?

Re 6: Are symbolic actions and rituals being used to support change? Are there, for example, any obvious, positive consequences, such as promotions or bonuses?

Re 7: Have we included enough feedback loops? Are qualitative project reviews held? Is there any direct feedback, e.g. from the "shop-floor", regional subsidiaries and plants? Are discussions with employees producing good results? Are process evaluations planned? Is there a standard feedback procedure following meetings?

Re 8: Does the overall architecture fit? Can it be changed if required? Have communication platforms been set up (e.g. steering group, sounding board, knowledge exchange groups, best practices, etc.)?

Re 9: Have we planned regular discussion sessions where the consulting team can reflect and build hypotheses? Are there any professional quality checks and feedback processes in place for the consulting staff?

Re 10: Do we fit the requirements profile? Do we continue to learn? How aware are we of our own strengths and weaknesses or hopes and fears? How strong are our psychosocial competences?

3.4 The Systemic Loop as a Basic Model

We already mentioned in the introduction that the "systemic loop" serves as the basic model for our consulting activities. The systemic loop is a simple and effective thought and process model that clearly illustrates the systemic attitude: "I want to understand what is going on. We have to begin by collecting information, building hypotheses and reflecting, not by taking immediate action."

The model consists of several steps, which are repeated over and over again to produce a better understanding of the situation: we begin by gathering information and building hypotheses, before moving on to the planning and implementing of interventions.

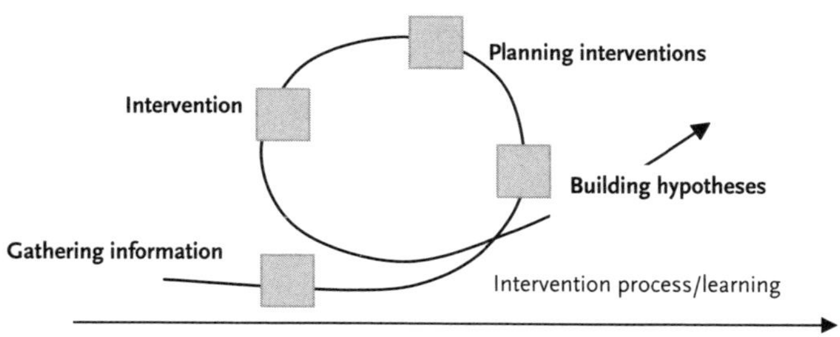

Figure 9: "Systemic Loop" Process Model

The loop plays an important role in a consulting project right from the very start. Projects of this kind always begin with some sort of conversation, be it on the phone or in a face-to-face introductory meeting. This conversation is followed by internal discussions and decision-making processes among the consulting staff. After the necessary information has been gathered, they begin building hypotheses, making suggestions and reaching agreements, then later introducing concrete measures, evaluating their effects, reflecting, discussing, adapting, and so on, until the project hopefully reaches a successful conclusion. Each project therefore has a beginning and an end. However, within this linear timeline, things progress not in a straight line, but along a "spiral" path.

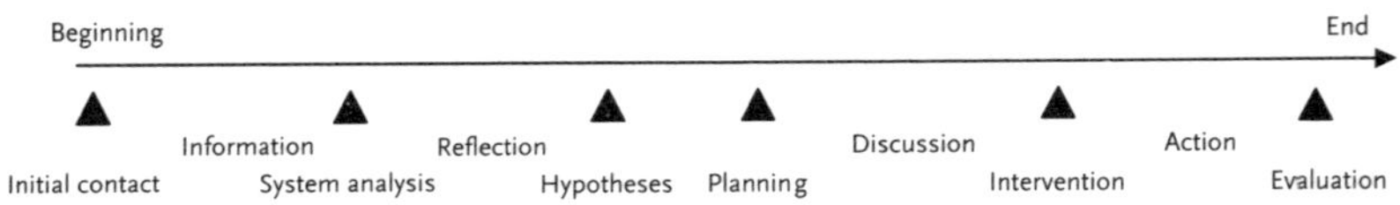

Figure 10: The Timeline as Basic Structure of Consulting Processes

If we take a closer look at the individual phases and steps in a project, we notice that the logic behind the individual steps and interventions always follows the same basic pattern. Each step itself contains the loop of gathering information, building hypotheses, planning interventions and intervention. Consequently, the step "Gathering informations", also contains the steps "Building hypotheses", "Planning interventions" and then "Intervention" itself and vice versa. This sounds more complicated than it actually is.

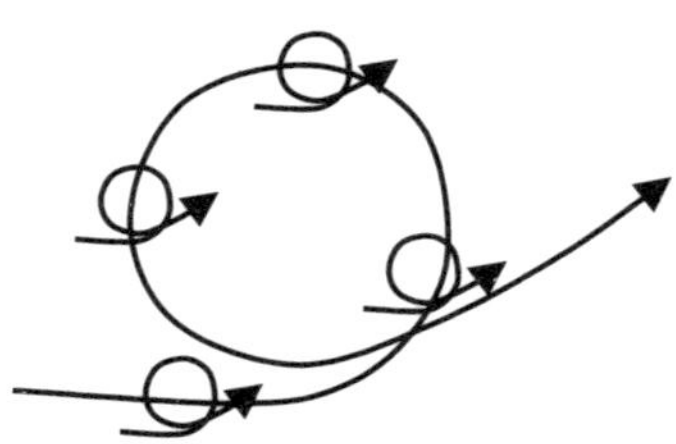

Figure 11: The Loops in the Loop

For example, when consultants ask questions in an initial contact meeting, they do so based on information they may have received in advance and on their own vague ideas and preconceptions of what the issue might be, what problem the client might have and what role they should play. At the same time, they also consider possible answers and consequences, build hypotheses and select appropriate questions. They are not simply creating for themselves a picture or snapshot of the organisation and the problem, they use this chain of thought to establish a joint "reality" with the respondents, a reality which will form the object of their subsequent deliberations on how to proceed.

However, it would be an illusion to believe that all we have to do to complete the picture is simply ask enough questions and gather enough information; in fact, we are always walking on a thin layer of ice covering a situation of great uncertainty.

The reflective, discursive clarification of the situation leads to assumptions on how to address the problem in the CLS. Thus, the hypothesis-building step is in fact also an information-hypotheses-intervention loop.

Although the client is involved in the reflective work, this part of the consulting process centres primarily around the consulting staff. Indeed, we would like to draw particular attention here to the significance and importance of the work that takes place within the consulting team(s). We find it impossible to imagine a high-quality consulting process that does not include this fundamental aspect. In a good consulting team environment, the way people trust each other and use their differences to complement and stimulate each other's ideas can almost be felt. The members of these teams listen to and motivate each other, competing in a constructive battle of wits not only for the best ideas and the best ways to put the message across, but also for pragmatic solutions. Finding the necessary depth of insight required for this work means regularly taking enough time to do so.

3.5 Hypotheses and Reality Construction

A central method in the systemic approach (integrated in the loop) is the building of hypotheses. This is a creative act in which fantasy and the ability to juggle with thought patterns and options play an important role, and which also requires great openness. Good consulting teams (COS) form the ideal setting and are a prerequisite for this.

In systemic terms, perceptions, experiences, conclusions, statements and claims are always *mental constructs*. What we perceive to be *true* depends on our mood, expectations, current situation and lifelong conditioning (cf. Königswieser 1987). The same applies to the things we remember, our past experiences and expectations for the future (cf. Ortner 2003a).

Seen in this way, hypotheses are "bridging constructs" that provide orientation and create a link either between the past and the present (i.e. memories, experiences, view of the world), or between the present and the future (i.e. expectations, hopes, intentions, plans). If something changes in this construed timeline, we seek explanations, causes and reasons. When we construct a mental image of what is linked to what and explain why something is happening, has happened or will happen, these constructs will never be totally free of our desires, fears and hopes.

When groups discuss different points of view and assumptions, the point of the exercise is not just to compare different hypotheses and select the one that can explain the most; it is also about finding and positioning yourself in the world, in that social space.

Hypotheses should be confused neither with attributing characteristics or qualities, nor with value judgments. For example, when a manager claims a member of staff is lazy, this is not only an evaluative description of that person, but also reflects their relationship. Such relationships do not have a clear, one-dimensional cause-effect structure and are therefore the subject of hypotheses such as: "These two people are not clear about each other's roles. They have contradictory expectations of each other. The structure of their working environment may well lead to this employee not being able to make the most of his potential."

Systemic hypotheses describe relationships, interaction, reciprocal effects and processes, they refer to different contexts, focus on resources and solutions and often seem unconventional. They try to uncover the hidden meaning behind problems. They have explanatory power.

3.6 Reflection

A further core process element in systemic consulting is reflection. Reflection literally means "to mirror" or "to give back an image", in this case in our mind. When we look more closely at this metaphor, we see on the one hand a process ("highlighting, reflecting, seeing") and on the other three elements ("sender, reflector, receiver"). When applied to thought processes, reflection means "to think about a thought", i.e. thinking a thought, formulating it in words, writing it down, establishing distance to it and "considering" it from an observer's standpoint. Why is this "reconsidering of our thoughts" so important in systemic organisational development?

When people argue or feel threatened by a difficult situation, even in unproblematic situations, they are always prisoners of these situations. When we are afraid, angry, sad, in love or in despair, we often do things without really being aware of our actions, things we might later regret and describe as "narrow-minded" or "rash". Similarly, something might at the time seem clear and patently obvious yet, when we think about it later, turn out to be the result of stupidity, infatuation or ignorance.

In simple terms, this means that each and every one of our thoughts is always connected to our entire body and soul. They have a reciprocal influence on each other.

Reflection requires distance, calm, "an ability to let go" and not always being "bent on getting your own way". Distance helps us to see things differently and to think. Joint reflection is a very useful way of verifying, correcting or even replacing trains of thought, patterns of thinking and routines.

Observing yourself, regularly reflecting on yourself, your thoughts and actions is so important in systemic intervention for one simple reason: it is only through reflection that we can verify whether or not our situative viewpoint and behaviour are consistent with the principles, attitudes, values and norms of systemic organisational development. Each question, hypothesis, action and reaction must be constantly verified to make sure it is not overly influenced by prejudices, preconceptions, emotions and self-interests that might blind the consultant to what is going on.

Reflection is a way of thinking that has to be learned. However, too much reflection can also result in inaction. At some point or other, you have to stop reflecting and act. The *basic attitude* required for systemic consulting described above provides both the necessary orientation and a safety net.

3.7 Feedback

The role played by reflection in the painstaking, individual process of thought verification is assumed in communication between people and sub-systems by *feedback*. Feedback is the mirroring of the effect of your own actions, broken by the view of the other(s). Norbert Wiener neatly summed up this point when he said, "I didn't realise what I had said, until I heard the answer". Feedback helps us to compare our own image of ourselves with that of others.

Although feedback can be addressed at a personal level in a systemic organisational consulting context, it assumes a role of lesser importance. Aspects of group dynamics and feedback in teams are, of course, also important, but they still do not form the primary focus of organisational learning and self-governance.

In our approach, we try to initiate feedback processes at those points where new patterns can be woven and second-order change is taking place (cf. Watzlawick 1974).

A good example of this are the feedback processes between organisational sub-units, e.g. headquarters and subsidiaries and their role carriers, which have no chance of occurring in the course of day-to-day business and via normal communication channels. Confronting headquarters with its image in the subsidiaries and with expectations of it that have previously remained unspoken can give rise to a whole new level of understanding. Although feedback of this kind naturally can involve hefty confrontation and emotional upset, it is nonetheless very effective. The actual feedback given might be targeted at sub-units and not at individual people, but it still follows typical feedback mechanisms.

There is no objectivity here either: individual assumptions, interests and self-portrayal play a role.

As Descartes reputedly once said, "What Peter says about Paul says more about Peter than it does about Paul."

Feedback is not always easy to interpret. For example, if a mother interprets a child's tears as a sign of aggression, she may scold the child. If, however, she interprets them as a cry for attention, she will take the child in her arms. This example can also be applied to organisations. If a production department interprets the expectations of their sales department as aggressive, as a criticism of the quality of their work, they will "hit back": "The sales department is a waste of time!"

If, however, they interpret them as a cry for help, both departments can work together on a new, joint solution to the problem.

Feedback is often confused with criticism, praise, recognition, humiliation or appeals for action. But it is not about assessing and judging, but rather about reporting back on the effects something has. Consequently, feedback should not be influenced by fears of triggering a negative reaction from the receiver. Feedback can only be given and received if a relationship is founded on a basic level of trust. It must never be misinterpreted as simply being presumptive. Once again, we find ourselves dealing with a paradox: trust is both the basis for and a consequence of qualitative feedback processes.

Feedback processes are always an emotional experience, regardless of whether the feedback is intended for us personally or in our capacity as role carriers, e.g. representatives of a unit or group. We suddenly find ourselves confronted with the image that other people have of us, and this can be particularly disturbing if this image differs from the image we have of ourselves (as is almost always the case). This applies both to unexpected positive and to unexpected negative feedback. But that is exactly the reason why the feedback instrument delivers valuable information; it can speed up development and steer behaviour.

The phenomenon that feedback sets a process in motion by which the people affected begin to continually modify their thoughts and behaviour is known as a "feedback loop". We have already mentioned that feedback loops are effective not only at an individual level, but above all at the collective, group and organisational levels. Individual feedback loops are important for individual learning processes, but they do not include a strong system effect. The real power of the feedback loops which lead to collective learning processes is set in motion by other instruments.

Many of the architectural and design elements described in this book serve to bring the different images of sub-systems into line and to clarify expectations. They initiate great processes of self-governance in a system. Consequently, feedback also serves to irritate the system and to reduce its "blind spots".

3.8 Observation Categories in Systemic Consulting

The above description of the individual process steps in the systemic loop raises a number of other question: How do we decide what information to select from the abundance of impressions collected while gathering information and building hypotheses? What are we actually looking primarily to observe? What is the focus of our attention?

A person with a mechanistic view of the world will ask different questions than those asked by a systemic consultant. All the factors mentioned in the discussion of the systemic view of the world, of organisations and of intervention can also be found in the observation categories we use at an operative level.

Once again, we have developed a kind of checklist to assist us here. It helps us to define the questions we need to ask and also provides orientation for interventions. Other questions will, of course be asked, based on any hypotheses subsequently built.

- What is the client system (CLS)? Where are the boundaries to be set?
- What is the consultant system (COS)? Who belongs to this system?
- What is the relationship between the COS and the CLS (CCS, contract, clarity of roles)?
- What expectations does the CLS have of the consulting project? What would constitute success? What experience has the CLS had with other consultants? Why do they need the help of a consultant now?
- Who are the relevant stakeholders? (Client, customers, suppliers, competitors, employee groups.)
- What kind of relationship does the CLS have to the relevant stakeholders? What characterises these relationships?
- Which structural and non-structural contradictions can be observed in the CLS and how are they dealt with? (Collective patterns of behaviour, problem-solving patterns, corporate culture.)
- What internal structures are in place? (Structural/process organisation; formal and informal networks, expectations, norms, rules; patterns of behaviour, rituals, games)
- Which of the internal structures reflect the organisation's environment? (Roles, norms, dependency structures, distribution of power, conflict dynamics).
- Who or what can be seen as displaying the symptoms of the problem (e.g. individuals, sub-systems)? What do they stand for?

- What function do problems and symptom carriers have and in which context? How have problems previously been dealt with?
- What do internal, informal relationships and latent power structures look like?
- What could be defined as the organisation's strengths and/or weaknesses?
- How strong is the pressure for change? (First order change, second order change.)
- What is the atmosphere, the mood like?
- What images exist of the future? What visions and/or strategies are available?
- How would the organisation's overall situation be depicted (metaphor, story, symbol)?

4. The Three Core Process Levels of Systemic Intervention

Three main levels of intervention form the core processes in our work: *architecture, design* and *tools*. All three of these levels serve to initiate organisational development processes.

The architecture forms the framework for the consulting process and can be compared to the structure of a house. The design can be likened to the interior furnishings or decoration of the rooms. The operative tools level corresponds to the fixtures and fittings, equipment and tools in the house.

Figure 12: The Complex Structure of a House

In the same way that Fig. 12 might be considered overly complex, our attempts to differentiate between architectures, designs and tools also often suffer the same fate. (The reflection loop is represented in the diagram by the bird's flight path.)

Before taking a detailed look at each of the three individual intervention levels, we would like to briefly present the basic goals of systemic consulting that in principle ought to be achieved through intervention (see Fig. 13):

- To secure survival and success.
- To clear the way for new or alternative attitudes and patterns of thought, perception and interaction; to facilitate new behavioural options and solutions to problems; to unblock energies; to break down rigid loops and inflexible structures.
- To reveal contradictory positions and remove the taboos associated with latent issues; to increase levels of reflection.
- To encourage people to think and perceive in systemic categories.

Figure 13: Goals of Systemic Intervention

The crucial difference between conventional forms of organisational consulting and systemic intervention lies in their respective intended learning processes: "textbook learning, specialised learning materials, recipes" in the former versus "social learning, learning to learn, life skills, the ability to develop" in the latter.

Systemic, social learning is not something that can be taught in a classroom or learned from a book. It requires special methods, procedures, techniques and tools. Systemic forms of intervention are extremely diverse because they are designed to intervene in complex systems and affect the complete spectrum of relationships between individual, social, structural, material, symbolic, collective and cultural factors in these systems.

4.1 The Five Dimensions of Intervention

At each of the three levels of intervention, there are always five dimensions to be considered: the *factual, social, time, spatial* and *symbolic* dimensions. The extent to which these dimensions will need to be shaped in a particular project will differ greatly from one situation to the other.

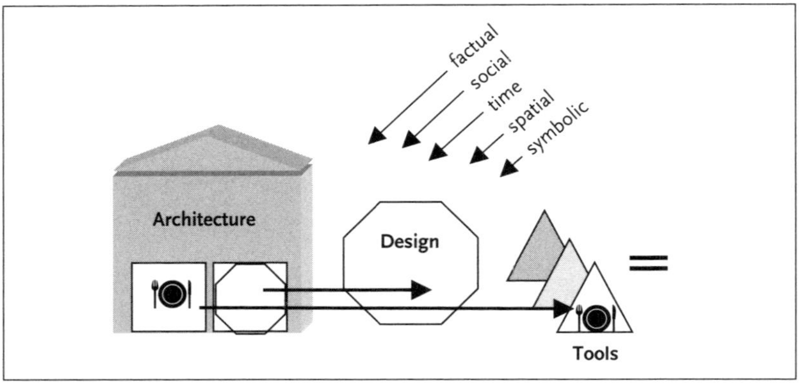

Figure 14: Architecture, Design, Tools/The Five Dimensions of Intervention

At the overall planning level (the architecture), decisions have to be taken on what the aim of the consulting project is (factual dimension), who the relevant players are (social dimension), how long the project should last (time dimension), where any planned events should take place (spatial dimension) and what form of symbolism might be appropriate (symbolic dimension).

Similarly, the focus of the design level also lies on carefully identifying the most suitable options. In the case of a workshop, for example, it is important that the goals are clear (factual dimension) and that decisions have been made regarding who to invite (social dimension), how long the workshop should last (time dimension) and the layout of the rooms/seating arrangements (spatial dimension). All such decisions on how to proceed are ultimately also symbolic signals.

The operative (or tools) level considers the actual goals of an intervention (factual dimension), as well as the target group (social dimension), the timing (time dimension) and the exact place to achieve the best results (spatial dimension). Once again, any decisions made at this level (the selection of a specific option) will also have a simultaneous, symbolic effect.

Whereas conventional approaches to consulting attach little significance to the symbolic dimension, the systemic approach places great importance on working with symbols and rituals. Symbols are social codes of understanding, and rituals are social codes of action. They both "get under our skin", i.e. operate at a level that affects our emotions, our individual and collective unconscious and our non-rational ways of making sense of something. Symbols are always something concrete, something we can sense. At the same time, they also have a deeper meaning only accessible to the "initiated". Despite all our technical rationality and scientific enlightenment, symbols and rituals fill and drive our social worlds and everyday lives: emblems and certificates, offerings and gifts, seating arrangements, welcome rituals, brands and even the clothes we wear. There is also symbolic meaning in our attitude to time. Making someone wait, for example, can be a way of signalizing power, position and influence. Non-verbal signals have a deeper, far more direct effect than spoken words or numbers (cf. Watzlawick 2000).

In the "Chance" project, symbolism is interwoven into all three levels of intervention.

At the architecture level:

- The make-up of the core group takes account of the different points of view found in the various hierarchies, functions and divisions across the company. This symbolises that everyone's perspective is respected and valued.
- Following the initial system diagnosis, the concept for the subsequent project steps is developed in cooperation with representatives of all relevant interest groups. This symbolises the great importance placed on diversity and cooperation.
- The restructuring of the planning process symbolises that the individual members of the management board share responsibility for the whole company, not just their own units.
- Informing everyone in the company that the management board is taking part in regular coaching sessions sends out a symbolic message that they are trying to "lead by example", i.e. working to improve themselves and acting as role models.

At the design level:

- The use of circles of inwardly facing chairs (without tables) symbolises that everyone in the group is of equal importance and that this is a hierarchy-free zone where people can interact without status barriers.
- Project reviews focus on "looking at now, looking back, looking forward" to symbolically emphasise the importance of reflecting, learning and breaking away from established ways of thinking.

- The "Market of Expectations" symbolises not only a willingness to listen and negotiate, but also fairness, transparency and a relationship of giving and taking.
- The "Values Diamond" transmits the message that values are something important, something you can hold on to, that they are long-lasting and enduring.

At the tools level:

- The "reflecting team" symbolises the following: We are for transparency. We have no secrets. The consultants value and understand the client system. They provide different ways of interpreting things, not ready-made solutions.
- "Analogue interventions", such as drawing pictures, using sketches to present examples, telling stories and parables or working with communication sculptures and constellations are used to symbolise actual situations, relationships, development processes and solutions.
- Even the names given to the individual intervention elements, such as "I have a dream" or the "Young Rebels" use linguistic images to transmit symbolic messages.

4.2 The Intervention Level "Architecture"

4.2.1 Basic Concepts

Although we talk of the "architecture" in consulting processes, we are not trying to imply this is some form of prefabricated construction that can simply be put in place, but referring instead to the planning and opening up of possibilities and areas for development. Just as architects design rooms and thereby create a framework in which all manner of things can take place, consultants identify the social, time, spatial, factual and symbolic design elements and the fixed points that provide the structure for interaction processes. In this sense, architectures can also be seen as interventions. Hypotheses form the basis of architectural plans and drawings, just as they do for all our intervention decisions.

Good architects draw up their plans in close cooperation with their clients, taking into consideration any global requirements and constraints such as general building and development plans, legal requirements, the surrounding area, the client's present and future needs, etc. As consultants, we do exactly the same, working in close cooperation with selected representatives of the client system to create an overall concept for the consulting process at the factual, social, time, spatial and symbolic levels. The same applies here: plans can change and may need to be adapted to suit the actual situation.

So what's the difference between architecture and design?

The architecture establishes *that* something is to take place and determines *what* that something will be, in other words it provides the headings, the cornerstones, the rough planning. The design determines *how* the factual, social, time, spatial and symbolic dimensions will actually look inside the given framework. As mentioned above, the design can be compared to the interior decoration, furnishings and décor of the building. However, since interior design ideas also have to be taken into consideration when planning the architecture and vice versa, the dividing line between architecture and design is often only conceptual.

The architectural elements serve a paradoxical function: they create the framework for open space. Consulting processes with a sound architectural basis facilitate changes in attitudes, allow multiple perspectives (e.g. through the use of heterogeneous groups), introduce new differences (e.g. through interviews with customers) and open up new observation, feedback or reflection possibilities (e.g. through elements like the "sounding board"). They facilitate the breakdown of entrenched patterns of thought and action, promote learning to learn and thus encourage self-governance.

Project architectures can be seen as the "higher school" of project planning. The ambitious development processes and complex problems addressed by systemic consulting require greater depth of process knowledge (see Figure 15).

Simple projects can be easily managed with classic project management tools. In more complex projects, the level of process know-how required increases accordingly. In large-scale organisational development projects, in-depth knowledge and experience of project management and process moderation are the basis for systemic consulting.

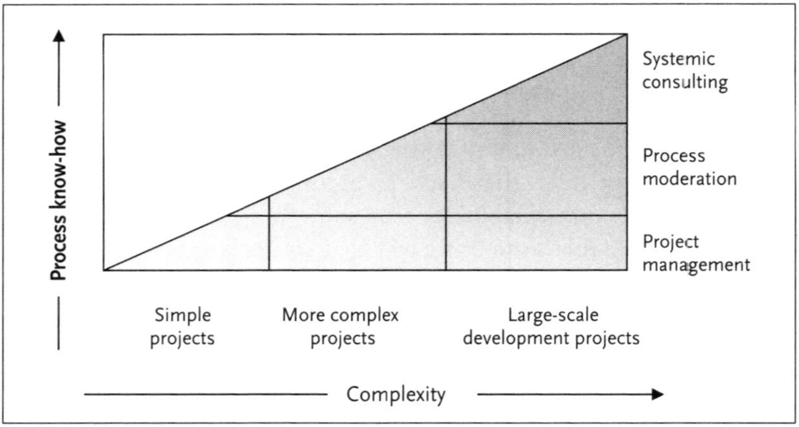

Figure 15: Project Complexity and Consulting Competence

4.2.2 Key Architectural Elements in Organisational Development Processes

The following architectural elements form the building blocks of systemic organisational consulting. They revitalise the system because they enable new forms of interaction and facilitate change in existing patterns. However, to achieve this and increase the ability of the system to reflect, it is vital that the consulting team is involved in designing and shaping these elements and then remain on hand to provide support throughout the process.

- **Clear Project Roles**
  Role of the sponsor(s): to initiate the project, set the strategic direction and goals, determine the scope and importance, allocate resources and act as a role model.
  Role of the internal project leader(s): to be responsible for strategic and operative project management. They don't have to do everything themselves but, by virtue of their role, are responsible for ensuring that tasks are completed to a high standard, in the prescribed time and using the allocated resources.

- **System Diagnosis/Evaluation**
  The system diagnosis provides the basic information required to construct hypotheses and delivers a deeper understanding of latent patterns and system logic. It is a form of intervention that

allows a system to take a closer look at itself. It also serves to build up trust between the consultant and client systems. Repeating the system diagnosis results in a process evaluation (cf. Froschauer and Lueger 2003).

- **Mirroring Workshops**
  In mirroring workshops, the consultants and clients reflect together on the results of the system diagnosis and discuss its relevance for the client system. They facilitate joint definition of the situation and thereby create the basis for a unified decision on subsequent steps, i.e. the consulting project architecture.

- **Core/Steering Group**
  The core/steering group is the driving force behind the change process. It assumes a reflective function and acts as a catalyst for triggering fresh ideas, launching new initiatives and motivating people to participate. This is the group to contact for any issues concerning the process.

  In its monitoring function, the core/steering group identifies and reproduces trends, moods and actions within the organisation and discusses appropriate actions.

  In its management function, it is responsible for initiating any necessary decision-making processes and ensuring the decisions taken are actioned.

  In its controlling function, it ensures feedback loops are included in the process and monitors the change process to assess progress, locate problem areas and identify any necessary readjustments.

  In its client function, it initiates sub-projects, prepares decisions and carries out internal marketing.

- **Sub-projects**
  Sub-projects can be used for drawing up concepts and preparing and implementing decisions. Creating sub-projects results in wider employee participation, thus improving the quality of the results and increasing acceptance of the change process.

- **Dialogue Groups**
  Dialogue between the steering group, sponsors and other stakeholders reduces the risk of the steering group getting "carried

away", losing touch with what lies within the realms of feasibility, or even developing into a parallel organisation in competition with top management. It provides both top management and the steering group with an opportunity to coordinate their opinions and activities.

- **Sounding Board**
  The steering group uses the sounding board to "sound out" the response and feedback from board members, employee representatives, key players and staff to planned initiatives. It can be used both in small and large group events, depending on the type and size of the project.

- **Large Group Events**
  Large group events offer an opportunity to reach large numbers of people at the same time. They help people make sense of what is going on and create a sense of community or belonging. They also provide an opportunity for direct dialogue, which in turn mobilises collective energy and speeds up change (Königswieser and Keil 2000).

- **Working with Internal Project Management Leaders**
  Continuous, ongoing work with the internal project management leaders provides stability to both the project and the process. It also helps the client system to build up process know-how and develop its independence. The project management leaders form an important bridge between the consultant and client systems.

- **Working with Top Management**
  "The buck stops here" and "leading by example is the only way" are two well-known sayings. Taken in our context, they highlight the fact that corporate management has to recognise what is going on and become personally and emotionally involved in the change process. Working with top management increases their awareness of the need for them to act as role models, set appropriate standards and play a key role in lending credibility to the project.

- **Teams**
  Most of the architectural elements described in this book are based on the assumption and experience that heterogeneous teams are the most productive way of addressing complex new tasks. We see them as an important element of self-organisation and learning in changing systems because they are able to pay adequate attention to and deal with the complexity of any internal and external influences. They are hyper-experts in dealing with complexity (cf. Königswieser and Heintel 1998). We find it useful to consider the four elements shown in Fig. 16 when building teams.

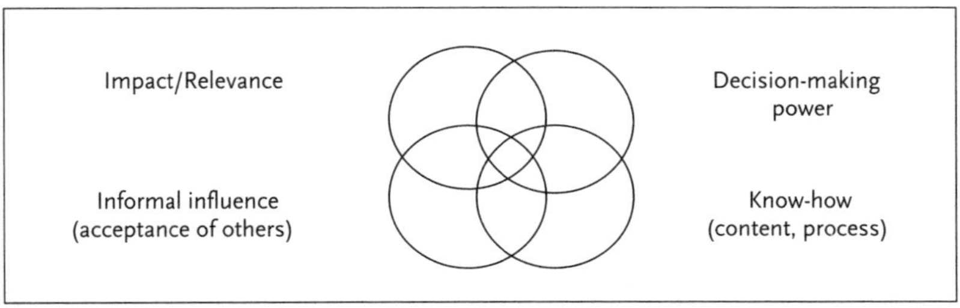

Figure 16: Main Criteria for Building Teams

An ideal team includes not only people with enough influence to ensure that decisions can be taken quickly on proposed concepts (if possible, the steering group should include a member of the management board), but also representatives of those directly affected to provide input on relevant trends and emotions. Ideally, teams represent a microcosm of the system.

If the group members also enjoy respect in key organisational subsystems, this will make their task easier and speed up the implementation process. People with relevant professional and process knowledge bring valuable system resources into the project.

Various other architectural elements will also need to be designed and included, depending on the goal and type of project. Examples include: multiplier fora, coaching programmes, train-the-trainer modules, departmental workshops and dialogue platforms. At this point, we would also like to emphasise the significance of the all-important deliberation work that takes place within the consulting team.

4.2.3 Architectural Elements in the "Chance" Project

The description of the "Chance" project in the introduction clearly shows how interwoven interventions actually are at the architecture, design and tools levels. The following list details some of the architectural elements used successfully in this organisational development project to initiate sustainable learning processes:

- the core/steering group (made up of people in positions of power, representatives of those affected, process experts and lateral thinkers)
- coaching for the management board
- repeated system diagnosis with location interviews/process evaluation
- the crash course in interviewing techniques
- the "Young Rebels" group
- the sub-projects "Vision", "Leadership", "Bureaucracy" and "Internal Communication"
- the leadership programme
- the project interviews
- the manager conference (large group event for 500 managers)
- the planning workshops
- the customer parliament
- the mission road shows
- the staff assessment meetings
- the site-wide events at the different locations.

Figure 17 shows the most important architectural elements used in the "Chance" project over a period of four years. This is a relatively simple yet effective way of representing complex projects.

The diagram clearly shows that:

- The project began with a system diagnosis and that the same instrument was then used for the process evaluation.
- Management board coaching was later integrated into the leadership programme (and thus held less frequently) since the entire board participated as a separate group in the leadership programme.
- As the driving force behind the project, the core group was the one constant element in the architecture.

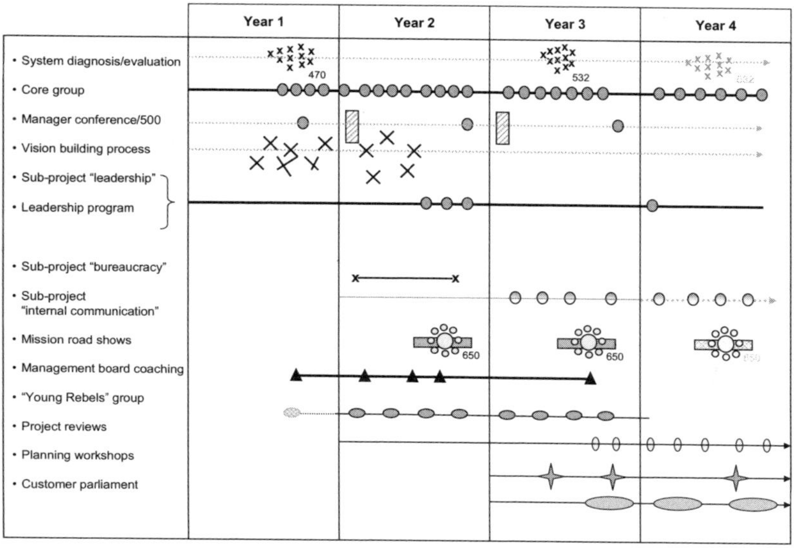

Figure 17: "Chance" Architecture

- The "Young Rebels" met and worked as a group for about two years.
- Project reviews were not introduced until year three, but formed an integral part of the project from then on.
- The new, improved planning workshops were not possible until the end of year two.
- The mission road shows were not initiated until well into year two of the process.

A further example of the architecture used in the "Chance" project was the leadership programme held in English for around 500 of the company's international managers. This sub-architecture was based on a customised process that builds on existing corporate structures. Important in such a programme is the inclusion of several different learning and development stimuli and the involvement of as many of the people affected as possible. Leadership programmes of this kind should also be closely linked to the change process.

The concept behind the leadership programme was developed in the accompanying project group (consisting of internal management representatives, human resources and external consultants). Based on the "Competence Wheel" model, the programme involved four three-day modules on the following topics: developing teams, systemic project management, conflict management and entrepreneurialism. Regional transfer rooms served as meeting places for sharing experiences.

Each learning group in the leadership programme (10 to 15 people) selected itself a project that it felt was "just slightly out of its league". All the projects conformed to certain predefined criteria and provided leverage for the change process. External project coaching was available if required. The results were presented in a special awards ceremony at a company-wide event. The whole programme was evaluated and provided – in conjunction with other architectural elements – an enormous impetus for change across the whole company.

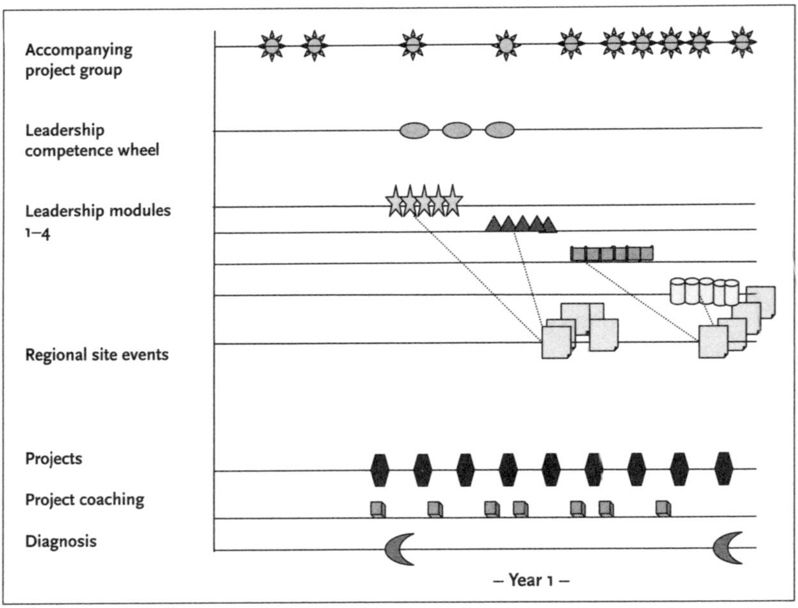

Figure 18: Leadership Programme Architecture

4.3 The Intervention Level "Design"

4.3.1 Basic Concepts

We use the term "design" to refer to the shaping and structuring of a specific step in the process, an individual architectural element. In conventional consulting processes, this is often simply referred to as the "programme", "procedure" or "agenda". However, systemic design processes distinguish themselves in the care they take to plan the design for all five dimensions – factual, social, time, spatial and symbolic – based on in-depth reflection and hypotheses.

There is often no real divide between the architecture and the design of interventions: they flow seamlessly into each other. For example, if we return to a pictorial comparison of architecture and design and imagine a door or large bookcase used to delineate two rooms, we see that these are both architectural features and at the same time interior design elements.

Designs can be highly complex (e.g. for two-day large group events), less complex (e.g. for half-day workshops) or simple (e.g. for 15-minute closing sessions).

Based on our extensive experience of projects of this kind and the goals of systemic intervention defined in Fig. 13, we have defined the following "rules of thumb" for each of the five intervention dimensions at the design level.

4.3.1.1 Factual Dimension

- Selecting the key factual issues is a highly customised process that is determined by the contract and its goals. This is fairly easy for manifest goals, although they can, of course, also change dynamically. It is more difficult in the case of latent goals, which often clash with manifest goals and thus cannot be directly achieved. We cannot place enough emphasis here on the benefits achieved by using analogue interventions.
- We place more importance on the actual experience than on theoretical input. It is much easier to bring order into experiences and emotions using explanatory models after people have actually experienced something themselves. That's why we avoid tedious group reports and plenary presentations. Wherever possible, we make use of information transfer methods involving some form of interaction, such as interviews, hearings, pin boards, etc.
- Where delicate issues are concerned, it is good to bring them out into the open from the outset and not make them taboo. However, it is better not to start working on these delicate issues directly and choose a more neutral issue instead, one in which the problems are bound to emerge anyway and can be dealt with more easily.

- Orientation guidelines should be established for a task right from the start, e.g. roles, timeframes, focus and methods. At the end of an intervention, everyone should understand the next steps, which should then be recorded in a written action plan. Closing reflections and feedback sessions are also permanent elements in the design process.

4.3.1.2 Time Dimension

- Less is often more. Stuffed, overloaded designs prevent people from relaxing, taking time out, reflecting and taking a deeper look at things. We often use delaying tactics like individual exercises, walks or meditation to create this time. Nonetheless, care should also be taken not to achieve the opposite effect, i.e. a programme that is too slow and not challenging enough. But this is generally the exception, not the rule.
- In a process-oriented approach, a clear direction must be defined and the start carefully planned (this is particularly important for establishing norms). The remainder of the process should then only be defined as a set of alternatives and the design subsequently adapted as required to suit the actual situation and based upon the careful deliberations of the consulting team.
- Since we really only give momentum to the process, and our suggestions and input are then turned into action by the client system (even when we are not there), we see breaks as "unstructured" work time where people continue the discussions informally and reflect on what is happening.
- Evening sessions are often particularly effective for discussing emotional, delicate or even personal issues. Such topics are also best dealt with in small groups.
- Timing is of the essence: a good intervention at the wrong time (e.g. too soon) will put people on the defensive.

4.3.1.3 Social Dimension

- Participant selection is carried out at the architecture level. As a result, the design makes use of any available working methods: plenary sessions (all the participants in one room), sub-groups (4 to 10 people), small groups (3 to 4 people), one-to-one discussions and individual exercises.

- Each form of interaction has its own specific effects, scope and characteristics. The art of successful design is to combine these individual forms in the best way possible and embed them in one energetic, harmonious final script. In the process, the actual decision-makers (e.g. CEO, project managers) should always be involved as relevant elements in their appropriate roles. In addition, each participant should have the opportunity to contribute as much as possible, e.g. through presentations, as co-moderators or in the preparations.
- Plenary events have the greatest potential energy, but also involve the highest risk. That's why we talk about the "fire" and special dynamics found in large groups. Splitting a large group into sub-groups for a particular exercise breaks down the "mass phenomenon" (Königswieser 2000).
- Small groups are sufficiently diverse to produce good quality results. Furthermore, groups of only three or four people also benefit from their intimacy, encouraging openness and trust and helping to reduce fears. People have the perception that their views really count. Individual reflection and consolidation exercises produce particularly high quality results in such a scenario. They help people to relax, yet concentrate and approach matters with greater intensity.
- One-to-one settings, e.g. two people going for a walk, provide an opportunity to discuss personal issues that are unlikely to ever be raised in front of a larger audience.
- Working on individual exercises encourages people to focus on themselves and concentrate on the essentials. We use them both to prepare for group work exercises and to reflect after public, joint work sessions.

4.3.1.4 Spatial Dimension

- While the selection of the location is undoubtedly an important element in the architecture, spatial arrangements also play a major role in the design. This applies to the way the room is set up (e.g. circles of inwardly facing chairs without tables), the seating arrangements (e.g. in a circle, theatre-style) and other items of furniture (e.g. pin boards, posters, podium, refreshment tables in the room or outside). It also applies to grouping arrangements within the room or to the decision to work in one room only, in breakout rooms or even in the open air.

- The effectiveness of some forms of intervention (e.g. the "reflecting team" or individual interviews with everyone present) is dramatically increased if the room has been properly set up, and the conditions are favourable. For example, if the view is obstructed or a room has poor acoustics, collective energy rapidly decreases.

4.3.1.5 Symbolic Dimension

The symbolic dimension runs through all the other dimensions. Symbolism attracts attention in each design element, as the following examples show:

- The decision on who to select to open an event or a kick-off meeting is usually made intuitively (typically the internal project leader, CEO or project sponsor). This signalises ownership and gives more meaning and body to the work that is to follow.
- Always starting core group meetings with an update session ("What has happened since our last meeting that could be relevant to our task?") signalises that transparency is the norm and that the group can only effectively reflect if its members are aware of what is going on and communicate with each other.
- We place great importance on designing special events to mark the completion of a project or acknowledge that a milestone has been reached. Celebrations of this kind are a strong symbol of respect, solidarity and recognition.
- Large group events are particularly rich in symbolism, since they are company-wide affairs and as such are highly charged with energy. What key players do – or don't do – in this kind of setting has a particularly long-lasting effect. Two years into the "Chance" project, the chairman of the management board publicly admitted he had underestimated its consequences and thus done little to contribute to cultural change in the organisation. This prompted a flood of positive emotional reactions, with comments such as: "It's all right to admit you've made a mistake here!"

During a management seminar, an irate board member handed the head of personnel a lemon as a sign of criticism. No words could ever have replaced the symbolic effect of this gesture. As a spontaneous design element, we invited the steering group onto the stage to reflect publicly on what had happened. This calmed the angry crowd and sent out a symbolic message: This group is able to deal with and reduce the drama in conflict situations.

Fig. 19 shows a simple set of steps that has emerged based on our experience in planning design processes. These steps correspond to the systemic loop shown in Fig. 9.

Step 1:	Collect information and construct hypotheses. What are our assumptions?
Step 2:	Set the direction. Where is our goal?
Step 3:	Establish possible modules, generate ideas. Which design elements are suitable?
Step 4:	Planning process/rough design. How should we create suspense? What does the script need to include?
Step 5:	Detailed design of the initial phase (with options for subsequent phases). Who should do what? When? How much time should be planned?

Figure 19: Design Process Steps

4.3.2 Design Elements in the "Chance" Project

Before we look in detail at some of the design elements used in the "Chance" project, we would like to briefly recall some of the elements mentioned in the opening chapter:

- team development
- project kick-off meetings
- building a vision
- sketches
- conflict analysis in the core group or management board coaching sessions
- qualitative project interviews ("learning, not assigning blame")
- stakeholder analysis/analysis of power structures
- interactive, experience-oriented design elements in the large group events
- feedback processes in the planning workshops
- negotiating expectations
- group interviews
- tandems
- working on values
- group work
- repeated use of the systemic loop.

4.3.3 Design Examples

The following examples of intervention designs represent only a small sample of the many options available. We have deliberately selected designs that have not previously been described in other publications, yet played an important role in the "Chance" project.

4.3.3.1 Systemic "Minilab"

<table>
<tr><td>Goal:</td><td colspan="4">To build up trust among the members of the group; to help them get to know each other better and more quickly; to establish a joint identity; to develop teams.</td></tr>
<tr><td>Number of participants:</td><td>3 to 100 people; many small groups (3 to 4 people) can be accommodated in one room.</td><td>Timeframe:</td><td colspan="2">60 to 90 minutes</td></tr>
<tr><td>Effect:</td><td colspan="4">As a result of the intimate nature of smaller groups, the type of questions asked and the limited amount of time available, a feeling of closeness, depth and trust is quickly established. People not only talk about personal issues, weaknesses and problems, they also reflect on what is going on, thus creating an atmosphere of respect. The limited time allocated for each question encourages people to "keep to the point" and leads to statements on core issues.</td></tr>
<tr><td>Comments:</td><td colspan="4">The trust established in each small group is usually also transferred to the larger group. Consequently, this design element can also be used for large group events. The timing schedule should be clearly explained at the start of event and strictly adhered to.</td></tr>
<tr><td>Additional fields of application:</td><td>Project kick-off meetings, getting to know each other exercises</td><td>Design:</td><td colspan="2">Traugott Lindner/Group Dynamics, as developed by Königswieser & Network</td></tr>
<tr><td>Step 1:</td><td colspan="4">The small groups sit closely together in circles distributed around the room. Each group assumes responsibility for its own time-keeping.</td></tr>
<tr><td>Step 2:</td><td colspan="3">The sequence of questions to be answered in each group is as follows:
• How did you experience the group-building process?
• What would a good friend say about you?
• What would a critic say about you?
• Your first day in the company: What was typical?
• What are your aspirations? Hidden desires? Fears?
• How open has the dialogue been so far? (Each group member writes a number between 1 % and 100 % on a piece of paper.)
Discussion.</td><td>
5'
5'
5'
10'
10'
5'</td></tr>
<tr><td>Step 3:</td><td colspan="3">The average openness value awarded by each group is announced to everyone (and the results noted on a flipchart). If necessary, include a brief introduction to the "Johari Window"[10] or the feedback process.</td><td>10'</td></tr>
</table>

Step 4:	The question and answer process continues in the individual groups. • What was your first impression of me? (Everyone selects two group members and asks them for their feedback.) • Who has had the biggest impact in the group so far? Everyone is given three "impact points" and assigns them to other group members. Discussion: What do we expect of each other, of good co-operation? • What do we want to call ourselves? What name would suit us?	 15' 10' 5'
Step 5:	How was this exercise (brief discussion in plenum)?	10'

4.3.3.2 Project Kick-off Meetings

Goal:	To understand and plan the project; to become a working team; to establish the professional and social make-up of the group.		
Number of participants:	3 to 20 people	*Timeframe:*	2 hours to 1 day
Effect:	The procedural steps in this intervention provide orientation on five levels: • Factual: What is our task? What are the success factors? • Time: When do we plan to reach a particular goal or milestone? • Social: What identifies us as a team? Who is responsible for what? What do we expect of each other? • Spatial: Where will we meet? • Symbolic: Name? Logo? Image?		
Comments:	The individual steps can vary in length depending on the specific context and overall time available.		
Additional fields of application:	Workgroup or departmental kick-off meetings	*Design:*	Königswieser & Network (enhanced approach to organisational development)

Step 1:	Welcome by the project leader, goal, agenda, organisation.	10'
Step 2:	Warm-up. What is my interest in the subject matter?	10'–30'
Step 3:	The client describes the project in more detail, explains the meaning behind it and justifies the selection of the team members.	15'
Step 4:	Project stakeholder analysis, market survey, hypotheses, opportunities and stumbling blocks.	60'–120'
Step 5:	Team development exercise, e.g. "Minilab" or outdoor training.	60'–120'
Step 6:	Planning. Definition of work packages, milestones, deadlines, resources and clarification of expectations.	30'–60'
Step 7:	Open issues and planning of further activities. (What? Who? By when?)	20'–30'

4.3.3.3 Analysis of Power Structures

Goal:	The power dynamics and involvement of the project stakeholders should be made visible from an early stage. Areas of possible conflict, but also opportunities for cooperation, should both be identified early and then concrete action plans drawn up.		
Number of participants:	6 to 10 people	*Timeframe:*	2 to 4 hours
Effect:	This form of intervention is particularly useful at the start of a project (or after achieving an individual milestone) for creating awareness of the level of influence exerted by the relevant stakeholders. This often reveals totally new and surprising perspectives, which in turn can lead to new hypotheses. These can then be applied to future work, thus improving quality. An analysis of power structures can also be particularly effective in crisis situations and at the end of projects prior to their implementation.		
Comments:	The aim of this intervention is to draw attention to the often taboo subject of power structures. Although this analysis of relationship networks is always a delicate issue, it is nonetheless also very effective.		
Additional fields of application:	Any context in which power politics play a role.	*Design:*	Königswieser & Network
Step 1:	Together, the participants draw a diagram of the relevant stakeholders and their influence on the project. In doing so, they consider the following factors: Who could influence the project's success or failure? How strong is their influence (different size circles)? How close are they to the project (distance from centre)? What characterises their relationships (symbols)?		30'

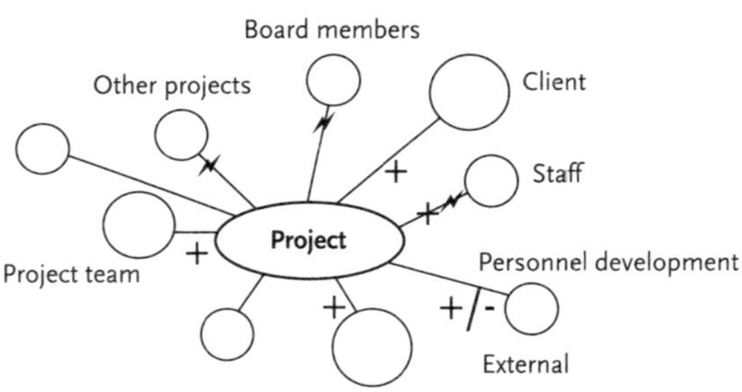

Step 2:	The participants construct hypotheses about the situation and use the diagram to discuss the influence and differing expectations that the various stakeholders have on the project. They put themselves in the stakeholder roles and look at the project from these perspectives. The identification of contradictory positions enables us to detect areas of possible conflict and take appropriate action.	30'
Step 3:	The participants then develop a specific strategy for each relevant stakeholder group that, in turn, leads to a concrete action plan. (Who? What? When?)	20'

4.3.3.4 Passing through the Time Zones

Goal:	To deal with unresolved issues and old conflicts ("tidying up"); to ensure people are aware of current issues and are open to the concept of working together for a better future.		
Number of participants:	3 to 10 people	*Timeframe:*	0.5 days to 1 day
Room requirements:	3 separate, clearly identified zones within the room to symbolise the past, the present and the future.		
Effect:	The physical and mental passage through the different (time) zones, briefly looking back (the past), taking a good look around (the present) and looking forward (the future), enables the inclusion of reflections and emotions. Switching between group sessions and one-to-one dialogue combines intimacy with more public discussion. Energy cannot be released for future projects unless old wounds are healed.		
Comments:	This design is particularly suited to teams with a long history of unresolved conflict, yet who nonetheless have to complete a common task and continue to work together in the future.		
Additional fields of application:	Site analysis, team development	*Design:*	R. Königswieser, A. Doujak
Step 1:	Following a warm-up and introduction, the participants work individually on the following questions: What was positive for me in the past? When did I feel hurt?		10'
Step 2:	The group positions itself in the zone designated as "the past". Each member of the group passes one after the other through this zone and, while walking, explains where they get stuck, where they feel strong, where they notice a tailwind, where the hurdles lie, what they can leave behind and what still remains to be accomplished.		30'
Step 3:	Walking in pairs. Theme: conflicts. What I have wanted to say to you for a long time... What can I contribute?		30'
Step 4:	The group then moves on to "the present" zone. The centre symbolises total satisfaction, the outer edges symbolise distance, dissatisfaction. Everyone explains their position and names their open issues.		30'
Step 5:	The group defines the current overall situation, constructs hypotheses and determines typical patterns in the way they work together. They devise draft solutions.		120'
Step 6:	The most important activities for all concerned are prioritised.		30'
Step 7:	The group then forms a circle around a positive symbol (e.g. a vase of flowers) in "the future" zone. Exercise: Let's assume all our wishes have been fulfilled. We tell each other how wonderful everything is (being as concrete as possible).		30'
Step 8:	Reflecting team. The external consultants provide their comments on the situation and the process of passing through the time zones.		5'

4.3.3.5 "In Tandem"

Goal:	To quickly reflect on and discuss (latent) issues, increase awareness and identify solutions.			
Number of participants:	6 to 18 people	*Timeframe:*	60 to 90 minutes	
Effect:	This design is also based on the loop model. The feedback and reflections of the sub-group (sitting in the outer circle and listening) contribute more to understanding and awareness than would be the case if the groups were to work in separate rooms and present their results at the end of the exercise. This makes it easier to raise awareness of latent issues.			
Comments:	Both sub-groups work apart and yet together, simultaneously and yet consecutively (with or without moderation). They sit in two concentric circles. The outer group observes the inner group and then provides them with feedback. The inner group are not asked to comment on this feedback, it is simply left to sink in.			
Additional fields of application:	Identifying latent issues	*Design:*	Königswieser & Network	
Step 1:	The participants split up into two equal groups.			10'
Step 2:	The first group sits in the inner circle, surrounded by the other group. The inner group discusses the issue or problem, builds chains of associations and hypotheses and reflects on them.			30'
Step 3:	The second group then replaces the other group in the inner circle and discusses their impressions of the first round. They then continue with their own reflections (with the other group now observing them).			20'
Step 4:	The two external consultants (as "reflecting team") summarise events so far and add their own impressions of the whole interaction process.			5'

4.3.3.6 The Project Landscape

Goal:	To analyze the status of a project, its processes and any positive or negative lessons learned; to learn from reflection and mistakes.		
Number of participants:	3 to 30 people	*Timeframe:*	3 to 4 hours
Effect:	The point of this intervention is to establish an overview regarding the progress (status) of a project, analyze the experiences made (pattern recognition) and learn from mistakes.		
Comments:	Open discussion in sub-groups takes the focus off individual "guilty" parties.		
Additional fields of application:	Identity building, team building	*Design:*	Königswieser & Network

Step 1:	The group is divided into sub-groups. The basis for selecting the members of these sub-groups is an (assumed) similar point of view. Key events in the past are then discussed, translated into landscape features (e.g. mountains, gorges, lakes, forests, fields, etc.) and mapped according to their positive or negative ratings.	40'–60'
Step 2:	Each group presents its landscape. The maps are compared and discussed.	40'
Step 3:	The group is then again divided into sub-groups, this time comprising people with different points of view. Discussion. What positive or negative patterns can be detected in the maps? What can we learn from them for the next project phase?	30'–60'
Step 4:	Discussion of results. Consequences are drawn and appropriate action plans prepared. (Who? What? When?)	60'

4.3.3.7 "I Have a Dream"

Goal:	To generate a positive image of the future, activate positive energy, strengthen confidence.		
Number of participants:	3 to 10 people	*Timeframe:*	90 to 120 minutes
Effect:	Picturing our own dreams in bold thoughts can both inspire and energise. Sharing these thoughts creates a deeper level of confidence and trust in both the community and the future.		
Comments:	Preparing a speech that lays out a positive future for the organisation leads us to implicitly describe measures which could turn the dream into reality. In this way, a collective image emerges of how this could be achieved. If there are more than 10 participants, they should be split into sub-groups.		
Additional fields of application:	Can be used in any context, e.g. identity building, team vision, etc.	*Design:*	Königswieser & Network
Step 1:	Individual exercise: Prepare a speech. Imagine how the company (department, etc.) would look in five years time if all your dreams for it were to come true (e.g. market position, customer relationships, staff, corporate culture, image, financial status, etc.). What would then make you proud to work here? What role would you play?		25'
Step 2:	Speeches (5 minutes each).		30'–45'
Step 3:	Summary: What threads or common points run through the speeches? What image emerges of the future?		30'–45'

4.3.3.8 The "Values Diamond" (Workshop)

<table>
<tr><td>Goal:</td><td colspan="3">To create awareness of the actual values practiced (in the organisation); to develop common, binding and viable values for all concerned.</td></tr>
<tr><td>Number of participants:</td><td>5 to 30 people</td><td>Timeframe:</td><td>0.5 days to 1 day</td></tr>
<tr><td>Effect:</td><td colspan="3">Sooner or later in a change process, the discussion generally comes round to "values" and other related issues, such as internalised views of the world and attitudes that are difficult to change. This intervention allows us to approach this difficult matter, in particular through its emphasis on common ground.</td></tr>
<tr><td>Comments:</td><td colspan="3">The focus here is the common debate on any values and attitudes that could be beneficial for company development (learning process). This is particularly relevant for top management, since the members of this group should act as role models.</td></tr>
<tr><td>Additional fields of application:</td><td>Team development, cultural analysis</td><td>Design:</td><td>Königswieser & Network</td></tr>
<tr><td>Step 1:</td><td colspan="2">Input on the subject of values (attitudes, views of the world, standpoints) as opposed to customs and norms; input on interview techniques.</td><td>20'</td></tr>
<tr><td>Step 2:</td><td colspan="2">The participants write down their thoughts on the following questions: What role do my values play in my dealings with my staff? Who do I consider to be positive role models with regard to those values most important to me? Who do I consider to be negative role models?</td><td>10'</td></tr>
<tr><td>Step 3:</td><td colspan="3">The participants split into groups of three (group members should have some sort of affinity to each other).</td></tr>
<tr><td>Step 4:</td><td colspan="2">The members of the groups interview each other (alternating between the roles of interviewer, interviewee and observer) on the subject of "values" and then visualise their commonalities (common threads).</td><td>15' each</td></tr>
<tr><td>Step 5:</td><td colspan="2">The groups present any common values identified to the plenum.</td><td>15' each</td></tr>
<tr><td>Step 6:</td><td colspan="2">Plenary discussion.</td><td>45'</td></tr>
<tr><td>Step 7:</td><td colspan="2">The groups each choose one delegate to represent them in the subsequent round of discussions. During these discussions, the delegates filter out 5 to 8 core values that should apply to future decisions.</td><td>30'</td></tr>
<tr><td>Step 8:</td><td colspan="2">The delegates sketch the "Values Diamond", which might look as follows:
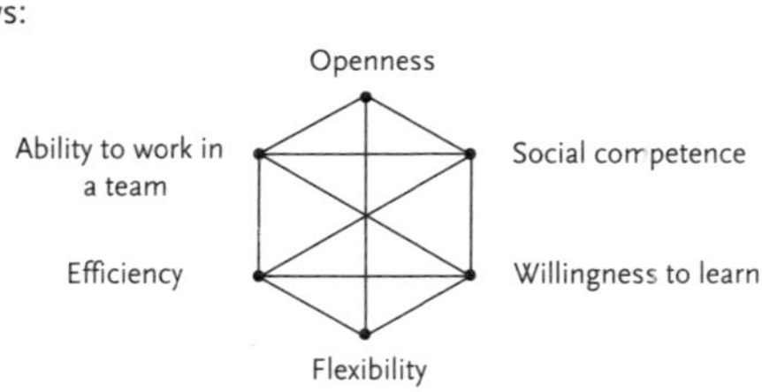
</td><td>20'</td></tr>
</table>

Step 9:	Turning theory into analogue examples. The participants form new groups and prepare sketches that illustrate the differences between the target and the actual situation with regard to values.	15'
Step 10:	General presentation, discussion and reflection.	20'–90'
Step 11:	The participants return to their original groups of three and provide each other with feedback. How do I see the others with respect to the aspects identified in the "Values Diamond"?	60'
Step 12:	The workshop concludes with decisions on the subsequent steps (e.g. restructuring of important meetings, job rotation, etc.).	30'

4.3.3.9 Market of Expectations – Improving the Quality of Leadership

Goal:	To determine what the individual sub-systems (divisions/key players) expect of each other; to improve the quality of leadership, enable successful cooperation and reduce the potential for conflict.		
Number of participants:	3 to 30 people	*Timeframe:*	2 to 6 hours
Effect:	One of the benefits of this intervention is that it is based not on a psychological understanding of the leadership role ("this person is a good or bad manager"), but on the assumption that leadership quality depends on the structural context and the quality of the relationships in that structure (clear expectations). Publicly negotiating the expectations employees have of leadership significantly increases commitment and the binding nature of any agreements made. We therefore strongly recommend that minutes are taken.		
Comments:	The clearer the mutual expectations, the better managers and staff can perform. Organisations often discover they have to create the structure required to enable lasting improvements in the way people work together. What is needed here are solid commitments, not just platitudes.		60'–180'
Additional fields of application:	Leadership issues, site-wide events.	*Design:*	Königswieser & Network
Step 1:	Introduction by the management representative. Seating arrangements: the members of the individual groups (divisions, teams) sit together around a table with a pin board behind them.		5'
Step 2:	Each group writes down their expectations of all the other groups (people) on individual cards and pins these cards on the board. Possible questions: • What should the others continue to do in the way they have done up to now (positive feedback)? • What should they change (criticism)? • What should they do that they have not done so far (wishes)? • What can we offer in return (proposals)?		60'
Step 3:	Each group then has the opportunity to explain to all the other groups (people, divisions, teams) what their cards mean. Mutual expectations are discussed, negotiated and written agreements made.		60'–180'

4.3.3.10 Site-wide Events/Hearings with Management

Goal:	To provide orientation, transparency, establish trust in management, clarify expectations, make plans for the future.			
Number of participants:	20 to 100 people	*Timeframe:*	1 to 3 hours	
Effect:	This intervention helps employees to voice important questions directly. Management has to accept the questions, ideas and expectations put to them and then address these issues as openly as possible. These face-to-face encounters create proximity between management and staff, reduce the potential for aggression and make it easier for both sides to understand each other.			
Comments:	The management representatives (1 to 2 people) should be briefed in advance not to react defensively. Employees should prepare plenty of questions, since experience shows most of them will be answered in the first hearings. The fact that these hearings are public events (i.e. open to the whole company) contributes in part to their effect.			
Additional fields of application:	Large group events, crisis situations	*Design:*	Königswieser & Network	
Step 1:	Welcome and introduction by the organisers; brief description of proceedings by the moderator.			5'
Step 2:	The participants divide into groups of 3 to 8 people (all the groups remain in the same room). Each group writes down their questions to management on cards (one card for each question).			15'
Step 3:	The management representatives move from group to group (10 minutes for each group), sit down in the group and respond to the questions on the cards. All the other groups listen to what is going on. This step concludes with the management representatives giving their feedback on the entire proceedings.			30'–60'
Step 4:	The focus now moves on to "the near future". Interest groups form and work on key issues with an emphasis on preserving what is good and proposing change. What do we need from management to achieve this? Each group's conclusions are then presented in plenum and agreements made on what the next steps are to be.			30'–60'
Step 5:	Evaluation: How do I assess the likelihood of this decision being implemented (on a scale of 1 % to 100 %)? Flashlights and closing comments.			15'

4.3.3.11 What I Admire About You/Positive Feedback

Goal:	To increase trust levels, improve relationships, strengthen appreciation.		
Number of participants:	4 to 100 people	*Timeframe:*	30 to 60 minutes
Effect:	Positive feedback establishes trust, improves communication and introduces flexibility into rigid patterns.		

Comments:	Positive feedback is a rare occurrence, negative feedback (criticism) is all too frequent. It is the moderators' task to ensure that participants keep to the allotted time and switch partners simultaneously to avoid confusion and lose the effect of this intervention.		
Additional fields of application:	Preparation for critical discussions	*Design:*	Königswieser & Network
Step 1:	The participants pair off and distribute themselves around the room. Each pair has a total of six minutes to tell each other what they admire and value about one another. No criticism allowed!		20'–30'
Step 2:	Change partners. Continue the positive feedback process. (Can be repeated as often as required.)		6' each
Step 3:	Short discussion in plenum. How did the participants find the feedback process? (Impressions only.)		10'

4.4 The Intervention Level "Tools"

4.4.1 Basic Concepts

Consultants have to be constantly aware that once the consultant-client system has been established, every subsequent action on their part will then be interpreted as an intervention, even when it is not intended as such. This also applies to every statement, announcement and comment they make or question they ask, since they are generally seen in the overall context of the consulting project.

4.4.2 The Intervention Tree

We have already emphasised the importance of the general framework surrounding the consulting process and of the manner in which an instrument is used if the desired effect is to be achieved. To illustrate this point, we often use the image of a tree. The relationship between the client and the consultant (CCS) is as important to a consulting process as the roots are to a tree. You cannot see them, but they supply the power and the energy. The framework, the architecture and the design can be likened to the tree trunk. They are the basis on which the various tools and techniques develop and come to fruition, like the leaves and fruit on the tree.

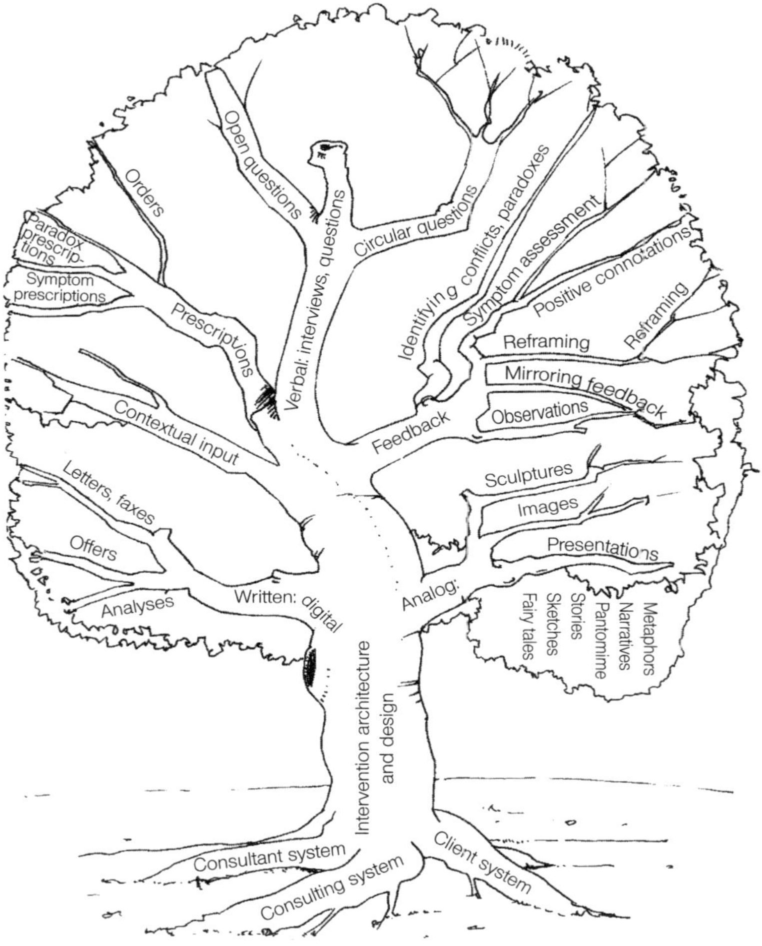

Figure 20: The Intervention Tree

We differentiate between two main branches of intervention: "digital" and "analogue" interventions[11].

Digital interventions can be further sub-divided into written and verbal interventions. Written interventions include proposals, slides, letters, faxes, flipchart notes, etc. Verbal interventions include announcements, requests, questions, instructions, tips, etc.

In addition, we also have a number of tools and forms of intervention with special meaning and particular significance in the systemic approach. Many of them have their roots in the traditions of systemic family therapy. As a consultant, you not only have to know and understand these tools, you also have to know how best to use them. Keeping notes of your own experiences and gradually building up your own "treasure chest" collection of tools is therefore a highly recommendable exercise.

The wide range of written and verbal techniques available are complemented by a specific *set of systemic tools,* namely "reflecting team", "positive connotations", "the good in the bad – the bad in the good", "reframing", "paradoxical interventions", "open and circular questions" and "splitting".

As discussed, the main functions of such tools are to penetrate ingrained ways of thinking and rigid loops, to clear the way for new perspectives and encourage the development of new forms of action through feedback. It is often difficult to draw a clear line between the individual interventions: they all complement each other and can be used in combination. But they nonetheless all have the same core function: to pinpoint new perspectives and help construct a "new reality" without exerting obstructive pressure for change.

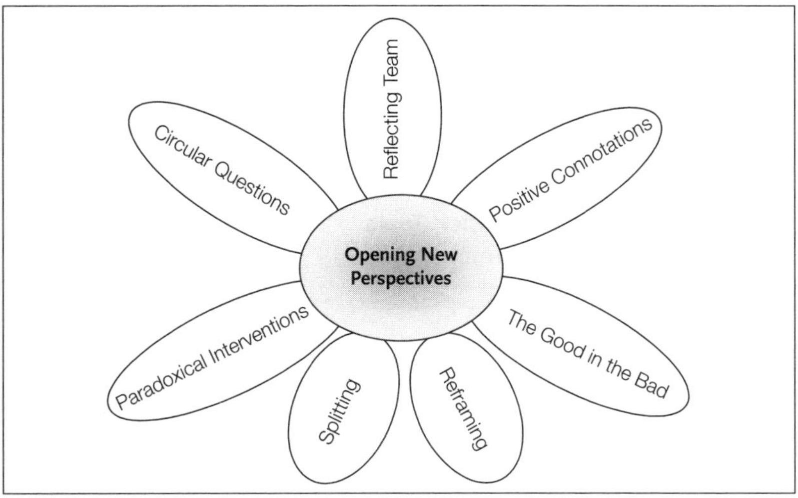

Figure 21: Specific Systemic Tools

All these interventions involve an element of danger or risk and using them can be compared to walking a tightrope. But herein also lies their potential for change, their extraordinary depth of effect. Such an approach is, in itself, not new: the words of wisdom encountered in the age-old Zen stories are full of paradoxes, reframings and reconstructions. Their "wisdom" comes from the way they reflect the paradoxes and inconsistencies of life and present alternative solutions to problems that go beyond simply "trying to engineer a result".

The notion that change begins in our heads, in our perceptions and in our views is also reflected in the common, everyday belief that "faith can move mountains". Letting go of fixed ideas and not necessarily trying to force change, relieves pressure, tension and fears. Accepting a difficult situation and even trying to reinforce it "paradoxically" by steering it in an unexpected direction can trigger new thoughts and release energy for change.

For example, if consultants send out a signal that a particular problematic behaviour pattern should in fact be regarded as positive, i.e. they see no need for change or even consider it undesirable, the desire for change in the CLS begins paradoxically to stir more than it would have done if pressure had been exerted.

Ultimately, the point is to de-escalate and de-dramatise the situation, and emphasise aspects that have previously been given less attention. Alternative points of view or new "light" on old issues can turn perpetrators into victims, chaos into creativity, oppressors into responsible citizens and fanatics into idealists.

How do we actually do this? How and when do we use these brief verbal interventions?

4.4.3 Systemic Intervention Tools

4.4.3.1 Reflecting Team

Field of application:	Creating awareness of specific system patterns and latent issues in front of small or large groups.
Effect:	The consultants let the group watch them while they carry out their reflection. Reversing the conventional direction of observation is like letting people take a peek through the proverbial keyhole. The dramatisation awakens curiosity, increases concentration and prompts reflection through its surprise effects (cf. Anderson 1990).
Comments:	This intervention has to be explained in advance. The chairs for the two consultants should be placed facing each other to allow a natural conversation flow; they should also be positioned to best suit the room's acoustics. The dialogue between the consultants should start on a positive note and then move on to hypotheses and feedback.

4.4.3.2 Positive Connotations

Field of application:	Often, positive connotations are not drawn in isolation but, for example, in advance as a sign of appreciation, retrospectively after kick-off meetings, mirroring workshops, etc., or in combination with other interventions. A positive reaction to a situation for which the system is already reproaching itself introduces an altered approach to assessing the situation and provides food for thought. Accepting a situation is the first step on the way to changing it.
Effect:	Appreciative feedback and imparting a feeling of being "really impressed" vitalises, spreads confidence, promotes trust and creates surprise.
Comments:	Finding the right words and making sure positive connotations do not turn into insincere adulation requires tact and sensitivity.

4.4.3.3 The Good in the Bad, The Bad in the Good

Field of application:	This intervention is used when the consultant system has the feeling that one side of a conflict is not getting enough exposure or, for example, if a situation is regarded as bleak and futile. There is usually less need to raise awareness of any negative aspects (when idealizing).
Effect:	Usually results in great surprise, an "aha" experience or a modified view among participants. Works particularly well in combination with the "reflecting team".
Comments:	When working on "good in bad" cases, care should be taken to ensure any worries voiced are nonetheless taken seriously. Similarly, opinions voiced in "bad in good" cases should not be seen as attempts to undermine the positive aspects.

4.4.3.4 Reframing

Field of application:	In situations with very complicated relationship structures, to determine victims/perpetrators, when it is clear that feedback workshops will be of no benefit.
Effect:	Reframing helps to create greater flexibility and self-confidence and thus increases the complexity of the whole. The contrary, often paradoxical view triggers feelings of surprise, irritation and positive confusion.
Comments:	It is only by expanding the frame of observation that alternative meanings and associations become plausible and applicable. (The well-known question "Is the glass half full or half empty?" can serve as a useful example here.)

4.4.3.5 Splitting

Field of application:	Conflicts between two parties; reinforcing two different factions in a group.
Effect:	The two consultants "split" their opinions and each adopt the stance of one of the differing factions in the system. Splitting the role of the COS creates an element of surprise, with both sides feeling their arguments are being mirrored and understood. The conflict is reproduced in the COS without consensus and is thus easier to deal with. A variation of this is the adopting of an "on the one hand – on the other hand" stance. Splitting helps the differing factions to reach a compromise, by showing them how absurd their conflict actually is. It is also useful in combination with the "reflecting team".
Comments:	Exaggerating the situation can create the opposite effect, i.e. an even deeper rift between the two factions.

4.4.3.6 Paradoxical Interventions

Field of application :	Particularly inflexible mindsets, rigid loops, resistance, situations in which the CLS does not respond to direct attempts to uncover the problem; not suitable in situations of great suffering (e.g. death) and heavy loss.
Effect:	The ambivalence between wanting and not wanting to change (double-bind situation) is resolved by the "counterparadox" in the message. ("Please don't change.")
Comments:	This intervention will always involve walking a tightrope between success and a cynical response from the CLS. If the consultant is not able to adopt the position required in a convincing manner, this form of intervention is better avoided.

4.4.4 Questions

Asking questions is one of the most important processes in systemic consulting. We ask questions throughout the entire consulting process: in kick-off meetings, during interviews and in all kinds of other situations.

The purpose of open questions is to collect information. However, in a systemic consulting process, questions are not used simply to gain insight into the relationship structures and complex sequences of action in a social system, they are, at the same time, also always interventions in that system.

From a systemic point of view, questions are *requests* to the respondents to carry out a selection "in their minds". In doing so, they differentiate between possible alternatives: "applicable/not applicable", "relevant/not relevant", "an element of/not an element of", "would classify as/is related to", "assess/explain with", "will answer/won't answer", etc.

In a "question and answer" exchange, the conditions, conventions, rules and structures applicable to general social communication space (e.g. good manners, morality, politeness, commitments and level of dependence) play as important a role as subjective factors (such as individual values, emotional state, life history, experience, prejudices and expectations). Answering questions is not a simple "computerised input-output" process. It causes a change in the respondent's cognitive, mental and psychological system.

Questions are used in all phases of a consulting project as an important tool for *steering* communication between the COS and the CLS. The format of the question and answer exchange depends on the actual task or problem.

4.4.4.1 Closed and Open Questions

We use the term "closed questions" to refer to requests for answers that form part of an existing joint framework of interpretation and can be answered with a simple "yes", "no" or one-word answer. These include dichotomous questions, multiple-choice questions and requests for information, such as "How many people work in the company?", "Is this your first organisational development project?", or "Is staff turnover high or low?" The respondent's attention is channelled towards certain facts and information. Basically, the use of closed questions avoids having to deal with new, qualitative information.

We use the term "open questions" to refer to questions that require respondents to make some form of declaration or modification to their framework of interpretation. Examples of open questions include: "How would you rate the company's position in comparison to its competitors?", "Where do you feel there is room for improvement?" or "Why do you think there are communication problems in the management team?"

Respondents are invited to express their subjective points of view, opinions and judgment criteria. Questions are not selected in advance. Although open questions also serve to establish trust between the COS and the CLS, their primary function is to ascertain the specific construction of reality, the logic that applies in a particular CLS.

4.4.4.2 Circular Questions

Circular questions are deliberately aimed at illustrating interpretation patterns and relationships, e.g. "How do you see the relationship between the team leaders and the department heads?", "What do you think the sales team expect of you in your role as head of marketing?" "Circular" in this context refers to the following loop: thinking, describing, reflecting, comparing, rethinking, reworking. When answering circular questions, respondents usually run through this loop in their minds as *expectations* and *counter-expectations* between hearing the question and giving their answer. "Thinking in this loop" brings barriers, taboos, hidden coalitions or aversions to the surface and enables us to perceive them in their changed form. By getting the respondents to talk about differences, about relationships between people and events, the system structure becomes recognizable at a meta level.

4.4.4.3 Interviews

Interviews are a special form of question-and-answer exchange in which both sides agree in advance to keep to the particular rules and roles of this form of communication. The interviewee agrees to provide information on the subject proposed by the interviewer, i.e. the interviewers select the topic of discussion, and the interviewees tell them what they think or know about this subject. A prerequisite for this division of roles is a difference in knowledge levels between the partners, a gap which should be closed in the course of the interview. In the case of factual knowledge or presumptions, the questioning will be like a court examination: precise and closed. However, if the aim is to gain insight into and better understanding of the interviewee's view of the world, value system and cognitive classification system (i.e. a qualitative interview), interviewers must take care not to foist their own personal view of the world on the interviewee by asking closed questions. Instead, they should endeavour to pick up on the interviewee's perception categories and differentiations.

However, open-question interviews don't generally follow a simple pattern whereby respondents openly volunteer information on what they think, what they feel and why they consider something to be good or not. Good interviewers have to try to place themselves in the position of the interviewees and understand their expectations.

According to Laing, people constantly think about others and about what others might be thinking they are thinking about others, etc. They ask themselves what others might be thinking and hope or fear that others might indeed know what they are thinking (Laing 1961).

The suggestions given in Fig. 22 are designed to serve as orientation guidelines for favourable or unfavourable question-asking behaviour in qualitative interviews:

	+	–
Behaviour	• archaeologist • openness, respect • curiosity, amazement • acceptance, admiration	• inquisitor • prejudice • knowing better • judgment, devaluation
Strategy, approach	• no fixed structures • openness, "w" questions • flexibility	• rigid structure • unity • standardisation
Techniques	• open, circular questions • listening • asking	• closed questions • leading questions • interruptions

Figure 22: Orientation Guidelines for Qualitative Interviews

This relatively black-and-white comparison illustrates the effect behaviour and a preconceived understanding of the roles can have on the actual flow of conversation. An interviewee is unlikely to open up to closed questions delivered in an inquisitory manner. However, an archaeologist's approach – appreciative and based on well-founded hypotheses – can be used to uncover the respondent's view of the situation.

The following section provides a set of guidelines for carrying out qualitative interviews.

4.4.5 Guidelines for Qualitative Interviews

- *Listen, don't talk; ask*
  "Please tell me more about that. You said 'usually'. What are the exceptions?"
- *Don't ask leading questions*
  Replace questions like "And that doesn't worry you?" with "How do you find that?"
- *Don't give advice*
  Replace "Talk to your boss – that should help!" with "What do you think you should do?"
- *Don't criticise*
  Avoid comments like "That was a bit stupid of you!"

- *Accept pauses*
  Taking time to think often helps us to understand better.

- *Open, evaluative questions or requests for information could include:*
  "What do you find positive here?" or "What do you enjoy?"
  "What do you find negative?" or "What gets on your nerves?"
  "What kinds of thing are rewarded/penalised in this company?"
  "Can you describe the relationship the company has with its customers and suppliers?"
  "What picture do you have in your mind of the company's future?
  "If you were granted three wishes, what would they be?"
  "If you were to draw a picture of the whole situation, what would it look like?"
  "Could you tell me about a typical aspect in the breakdown of the relationship?"

4.4.6 Guidelines for Using Circular Questions

If open questions are the basis, then circular questions must be the "art" of asking questions. To illustrate this point, we have put together a list of some of the circular questions we find particularly useful for revealing and explaining differences. However, one thing is certain: examining the differences is always an excellent way of uncovering qualitative information.

- *The Absent Present*
  These questions reveal invisible influences, pinpoint relationship patterns and highlight assumptions made about others.
  "How would the new CEO describe the situation?"
  "What would the customers say about that?"

- *Ranking Questions*
  Ranking questions are used to reveal differences.
  "Who do you value most/least as a colleague/member of the board?"
  "Which part of the company has the best image?"

- *Percentage Ratings*
  Percentage questions invite respondents to clearly assess ideas, convictions, opinions and moods by asking them to rate their responses on a percentage scale.

"How strongly would you rate the department's defence mechanisms on a scale of 0 % to 100 %?"
"The company is facing a crisis. How strongly do you agree with this statement on a scale of 0 % to 100 %?"

- *Relationships*
  Relationship questions are used to find out who "gets on better" with whom by inviting third parties to "gossip" about or give their view of other people's relationships.
  "Where are the coalitions in the company?"
  "How would manufacturing describe the relationships between the different sales units?"

- *Expectations*
  Asking people about their expectations helps clarify relationships, such as the context of a contract and people's expectations of it.
  "Whose idea was it to contact us?"; "Why now in particular?"
  "What do we have to do to meet your expectations"; "What would make you see the consulting project as a success or a failure?"
  "How does the problem affect you?"; "How would you know it had been resolved?"
  "How do you explain the reasons for the problem?"
  "What has changed in your relationship to customers since the problem first arose?"

- *Constructing Possibilities: Solution and Problem-oriented Questions*
  These questions help people to elaborate their own possible solutions.
  "What would be a good solution?"
  "You wake up one morning and the problem is gone. What has changed? (The "miracle question".)
  "What would change in the company if the problem were to disappear?"
  "What could you do to initiate a change?"

- *Aggravating the Issue*
  Asking aggravating questions emphasises the functional side of problems and reduces them to absurdity.
  "Who would have to do what to make the problem even worse?"
  "What would suffer if the problem were to disappear"; "Who or what might benefit from the problem being around a bit longer?"

4.4.7 Guidelines for Initial Meetings

During initial contacts with potential clients, the use of "questions" as an intervention form assumes particular importance. It is at this stage that an overview of the situation is formed and the working relationship between the CLS and the COS, i.e. the CCS, is forged. Like the basic melody in a musical composition, the patterns of behaviour within the CCS are now set. Every consultant needs to find a way of doing things that suits their own personality. The following checklist for asking questions illustrates the way we handle such an intervention.

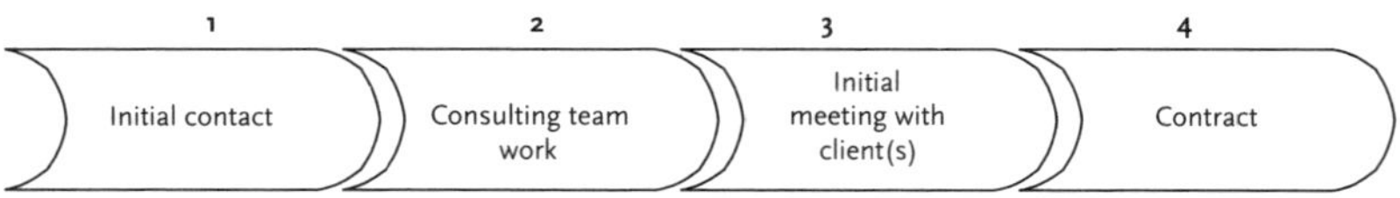

Figure 23: Procedure for Initial Meetings

- *Initial contact (usually by telephone)*
  What's the problem?
  Who is the caller? (Role, position in the company, length of service)
  Key facts and figures about the company (hard facts: products, size, number of employees, turnover, profitability, etc.)
  Why did you contact me/us in particular?
  Gather important background information. (How did the potential client find out about us?
  What image and/or expectations does the client have of us?)
  Why are they now considering the consultancy option?
  What triggered this process?
  Whose problem is it?
  Who is for/against a possible consulting project?
  Are they calling on their own initiative or did someone else ask them to contact us?
  What are the effects of the problem?

- *Plan the next meeting (normally the initial meeting):*
  What should be the goal of the meeting?
  Is it about "getting to know each other", gathering information and/or decision-making?
  Who will/should participate? (As many decision makers as possible.)

Will one or two consultants be required? (Two is preferable.)
Where will the meeting take place? At an external location? At the client's site? (Advantage: we can gather more information about the company.)
Is the initial meeting free of charge or will it be billed?
Will travel expenses be covered?
How much time is planned? (Typically 90–120 minutes.)
Who will open the meeting and make the introductions? (Preferably our contact.)
Will information material be sent in advance?

- *Confirm the appointment by e-mail, mail or fax.*

- *Consulting Team Activities*
  A COS, ideally two consultants, is now formed for an as yet relatively unclear CLS.
  Consulting team members: Which consultants should work together? Criteria: ability to connect with people, work well as a team. Who will assume the lead role? (Usually the consultant initially contacted by the client.) How are the roles to be divided?
  Hypotheses: The consulting team builds hypotheses based on the initial telephone conversation with the client. Further information on the CLS can be gathered through, for example, an internet search.
  The exact procedure for the initial meeting always needs to be discussed in advance and adapted to suit the actual situation. A telephone call shortly before the meeting helps to cement the relationship and allows last minute details to be discussed.

- *Initial client meeting:*
  Clarification of goals, warm-up:
  The client (contact person) opens the meeting, welcomes the participants, explains the background to the meeting, its aims, the timeframe and planned procedure.
  The consultants then describe the goals and procedure from their perspective.
  Important: It should be clear from the outset that, at the end of the meeting, the consultants might either retreat to discuss

the possible project procedure among themselves, or remain in the room and discuss their impressions and reactions in the presence of the CLS.

Discussion of the situation and problem:

Begin with an information-gathering phase using open and circular questions:

What is the situation?

What would other people say if they were here?

Who needs the consulting services?

Who is the target for the consulting?

What has already been tried?

Are any other consultants currently working with the client?

What are the (different) expectations and aims?

What should or should not be achieved by the process?

What would constitute a success from the various perspectives?

How will the client recognise that he has been well advised?

Clarify timeframe and role expectations.

The observation criteria and checklists for asking questions provide further assistance.

Building of hypotheses within the consulting team (either in another room or in the presence of the CLS):

Initially, reactions and responses are discussed and positive connotations identified; hypotheses are constructed and a draft architecture developed.

If this is done in the presence of the CLS, it automatically includes the mirroring aspect. This is a very delicate situation, since it is at this juncture that the course for the project is set and the CCS established.

Determine the reactions of the CLS by asking the following questions:

What are your reactions to our discussion?

What do you think of our proposed concept?

(The CLS is usually impressed by this intervention.)

Planning meeting:

Discuss the draft architecture and establish a possible plan of action.

Discuss client resource requirements (time, cost, effort).

What are the next steps?

When a CCS is formed, the following roles have to be assigned: main contact, project leader(s) and suitable team members (including people in positions of influence, experts, employees affected by the process).

- *Written quotation*
  Larger contracts may require several meetings with the CLS and internal consulting team sessions before a detailed quotation can be prepared. Although a written quotation should always be provided, it is preferable for it to be presented and explained in person. The main points, such as starting situation, goals, planned activities, architecture diagram, costs, project organisation, principles, approach, references and terms and conditions must be clear and precise, i.e. in terms clearly understandable by the CLS.

- *The contract*
  Once the quotation is signed, the contract becomes valid and the CCS is formed.

4.4.8 Analogue Intervention Tools

If we briefly return to the layout of the intervention tree shown in Fig. 21, we notice a branch representing "analogue interventions" on the right-hand side of the tree.

We see analogue interventions as holistic instruments which address people's emotions and experiences, get them to "open their hearts", and set bells ringing at a deeper, emotional, subconscious level. We have already mentioned the very special effect this "artistic" form of intervention can have in our discussion of the "symbolic dimension of intervention". For example, recounting fairy tales can be a far better way of describing the latent aspects of organisational culture than a rational analysis.

There is a vast range of variants and combinational possibilities for a metaphorical, allergorical and symbolic representation of reality. Time and again, we find ourselves fascinated by the levels of creativity people show in presenting their own situation in analogue form. Getting people to use these presentation techniques themselves is far more effective than watching an external consultant draw pictures or listening to them telling stories. The images people create for themselves are rooted far more deeply in the experiences and emotions of their creators.

We use analogue interventions in a whole range of different situations, as the following examples show. To mirror the results of a diagnosis, we present the images given in the interviews. The members of a steering group write stories about how they think the company will look in three years time or describe the path they will need to follow to reach that point. Following merger processes, constellations and communication sculptures serve to clearly (and emotionally) pinpoint the relationship between the two companies involved. Encouraging people to paint pictures, make videos or present short plays or sketches invariably releases strong emotions: the process of self-observation, self-presentation and building feedback loops raises collective awareness of "blind spots".

Analogue forms of intervention integrate contradictory positions better than any other form of intervention. They illustrate the emotional drama of a situation and do not detract from internal conflicts, but instead serve to express fears, longings and development possibilities with appropriate symbolism. Analogies are at their most gripping when they are used to translate latent issues, bring hidden problems out into the open and offer people something they can identify with. Consequently, analogue interventions are far more tricky and delicate than their "digital" counterparts. However, the risks are worth it if you want to achieve a far-reaching effect.

We don't see any real benefit in listing any more examples of analogue interventions used in the "Chance" project than we have already done, since it is not really possible to convey their effect when they are taken out of their actual context. Instead, we will limit ourselves to the following Zen story told to us by a client with the comment: "That's how I felt during our consulting process!"

Hear the Unheard

"King Ts'ao sent his son, Prince T'ai, to the temple to study under the great master Pan Ku. Pan Ku was to teach the young prince all he needed to know to become a good ruler. When the prince arrived at the temple, his master sent him out alone into the Ming-Li Forest. He was to remain there for one year and then return to the temple and describe the sound of the forest. Upon his return, the prince said, "Master, I could hear the cuckoos call, the leaves rustle, the hummingbirds hum, the crickets chirp, the grass sway, the bees buzz and the wind whistle." When the prince had finished, his master sent

him back out into the forest and told him to listen more closely, a request that puzzled the young prince. "Had he not already heard every sound there was to hear in the forest?"

Day after day and night after night, the prince sat alone in the forest and listened. But he could hear no other sounds than those he had already heard. One morning, the prince was sitting silently under the trees when suddenly he began to recognise faint sounds that were unlike anything he had ever heard before. The more closely he listened, the clearer they became. A feeling of enlightenment came over him. "These must be the sounds my master wanted me to perceive", he thought. "When the prince arrived back at the temple, his master asked him what else he had heard. "Master," answered the prince respectfully, "when I listened very carefully, I was able to hear things I had never heard before – the sound of flowers opening, the sound of the sun warming the earth and the sound of the grass drinking the dew." The master nodded approvingly. "To be a good ruler," Pan Ku remarked, "you have to be able to hear the unheard."

4.5 Examples of Tools used in the "Chance" Project

We know that it is often difficult to picture the intervention forms described above. However, to help us in doing so, we have to take another look at the case study (since we are now all quite familiar with the context). Which interventions are mentioned at the tools level?

4.5.1 Reflecting Team

We use this form of intervention regularly. It is part of our established repertoire and a kind of ritual in our work.

Situation: Restlessness in the room, mobile phones ringing, people going in and out.

Result of our deliberations: "The people here are under real pressure. They obviously have a very strong sense of responsibility, because they cannot switch off from their tasks and commitments even here. Perhaps we should plan in a few more breaks."

Situation: The evaluation results presented in a mirroring workshop are totally rejected by the core team. "That can't be right! We have changed far more over the last year than is being mirrored here!"

Result of our deliberations: "It must be terrible to go through all that change and yet still be shown yesterday's face in the mirror. The enormous efforts these people have put into this project are obviously not reflected sufficiently in the study. This process evaluation might have been correct six months ago, but it is obviously wrong now". (Months later, this evaluation was presented company-wide as the "truth"!)

4.5.2 Reframing

There are many different examples of reframing.

Situation: Constant talk of problems and complaints about "how bad the situation is". No mention of any positive or successful aspects unless prompted several times.

Our comment: "This group seems to set very high standards for itself. That's why they focus primarily on difficulties, on things they have not yet achieved. They never let themselves relax. They have an almost heroic attitude to duty."

Situation: One monologue after another. Speeches are enervating and far too long, yet nobody intervenes. Non-verbal signals indicate no-one is listening any longer.

Our comment: "Making yourself heard is obviously difficult in this company. That might be why everyone hogs the podium: they are making sure they're heard."

Situation: Aggressive, competitive behaviour between members of the different companies in the group. Similar battles also take place in the core group and in sub-projects.

Our comment: "We're impressed by the high degree of loyalty to the individual home systems, which causes people here to fight with each other."

4.5.3 Analogue Interventions

Initial scepticism was later replaced by enthusiasm.

Situation: A picture of the current situation is presented (a fleet of individual ships in intermittent radio contact with each other).

Intervention: We encourage people to talk about differences and commonalities between the groups, between their present situation and their wishes for the future.

Situation: The first module in the leadership programme almost failed. The core group has to decide whether to continue the programme or not.

Intervention: We tell them a story about kings and princes, court assemblies, rivalries, uncertainties and transformations.

Situation: Poor management is like a "red rag" to a bull. They are to blame for everything.

Intervention: We ask people to perform sketches to illustrate management today (scenes showing partisanship, inconsistency, conflict avoidance); management tomorrow (scenes showing professional, well thought out, consistent behaviour).

Situation: The individual companies in the group compete more with each other than they do with external competitors. "We act as if the enemy were in our own midst, not somewhere else."

Intervention: We use a communication sculpture to represent the relationships between the different units. Although the result is frightening, it in fact shows nothing new and people already had a vague idea of how tense relationships actually were.

Situation: The "vision-building" process is completed. How will the results be accepted?

Intervention: We try out a short role-playing exercise. "What would the members of the supervisory board, the subsidiaries, the customers, etc. say about this vision?"

5. Difficult Situations

What each individual classifies as a difficult situation in the consulting process is, of course, relative and differs from person to person. Does "difficult" refer, for example, to the reaching of contractual goals, to problems in the COS or to the relationship between the CLS and the COS? In this chapter, we examine ten problematic situations either commonly encountered in our projects or which have triggered a feeling of helplessness or uncertainty in the COS during our training programmes or supervision activities. The ten difficult situations we have chosen are as follows: resistance to change, escalating conflicts, threat of stoppage of the consulting project, no top management support, an unexpected crisis in the CLS (e.g. people have to be made redundant), power struggles, lack of resources, dealing with "rigid loops", no basic understanding of the process-oriented approach or when the consultants are not taken seriously.

Situations are usually defined as difficult or problematic when they give us the feeling of perhaps being out of our depth. Nevertheless, it is important to remember that it is often the difficult situations that in fact provide the momentum for organisational development processes. We often discover – and this applies to ourselves as well – that problems take on new meaning when they are looked at from a different perspective. We already considered this aspect in the discussion of systemic attitude in Chapter 3.

What applies to the CLS also applies to ourselves as consultants: before we can make a well-founded decision on the most suitable interventions to use in a difficult situation, we must first analyze the context and form solid hypotheses. The situations described here are based on our own experience and the ideas discussed are intended simply as basic guidelines or "rules of thumb".

5.1 "We face resistance, what should we do?"

Resistance is energy. It can be open and manifest or hidden and latent. It is always an indication that a system is afraid of either loss or too rapid change. Systemic consultants often reject the notion of resistance as inadmissible. "If resistance is encountered, the consultants must have done something wrong." We take a less radical view and, after careful analysis of the situation, generally advise people to respect this energy and look upon and promote it as positive. This attitude alone often helps to unblock a difficult situation. Resistance seems to us to be used as a collective term for all manner of different phenomena all indicating the same: things don't always go the way we want them to.

Resistance can manifest itself in many ways, including the following:

- Our process suggestions are rejected: "We don't need large group workshops; we can inform people in writing about the need for change."
- The steering group revolts against the process: "The whole process is too risky; future decisions should be based only on facts and not on soft issues like feedback."
- Important interventions are boycotted: "These reflection sessions take far too much time; we have work to do as well."
- A need to be seen to be doing something, defending one's territory: "We have so much to do, we won't be able to participate regularly."
- Plenty of talk of support, but no action: "As board members, it is up to us to change the way we manage things and act as role models." Yet no personnel decisions follow to help achieve the desired changes in behaviour and back up this statement.
- Intrigues and underhand behaviour. Although the official line supports cultural change, attempts are at work behind the scenes to undermine the "driving forces" even using underhand means: "I heard that not even the project manager really believes it can work. He's only interested in furthering his own career."
- Rational arguments citing, for example, reasons of time and money are often used as an indirect expression of resistance: "Of course we realise we have to work at learning from our mistakes, but we just don't have enough time. We have more important things to do and the consulting process is too expensive."

5.2 "Conflicts escalate and we find ourselves in the middle."

Change normally does not happen without conflict. Conflicts bring to light the differences and opposing poles in power dynamics. It is not uncommon for people to try to use consultants to further their own interests. In situations like this, we have to try to remain neutral, encourage dialogue between the conflicting parties (e.g. purchasing and sales) and offer them the support they need to find a common solution to the problem. A number of different designs can be used here, depending on the context.

Handling conflicts with confidence also requires the ability to deal with your own fears, calm a situation down and win the acceptance of all parties involved. As one client commented: "You were not intimidated by the situation. That helped us resolve our conflict."

Understandably, the situation becomes particularly difficult when the COS finds itself trapped between the fronts or even "blamed" for the situation and used as a scapegoat.

Conflicts within the consulting team are no less difficult. They might be the result of rivalry between the individual team members (e.g. external and internal consultants, traditional and process consultants) over who has the lead, who earns the most money, who can build up the most relationship capital in the CLS, etc. The more consultants reflect about themselves, the better they are able to deal with such situations.

5.3 "The future of the project is threatened, but we really need it to continue."

In all change processes, strategic decisions may need to be taken that could ultimately also threaten the future of the consulting project. We always have to be aware of this possibility. Generally speaking, it is also an indication that something is really beginning to happen in the system.

If consultants are economically dependent on a project, they may find it difficult to remain calm when such a situation arises. That is why a basic level of economic independence is an important prerequisite for consulting professionalism. Of course, when you are still establishing your customer base, this leaves you facing a paradox, and how one resolves this situation is something one has to decide for one's self. Having the freedom to decide when a project still makes sense or when it might be better to withdraw from the client system is not a luxury to be kept for exceptional circumstances: it is a question that has to be asked periodically in every project. In many cases, seeing the situation clearly and setting the necessary limits requires personal awareness of the framework needed for success. For example, signalizing a willingness to stop the project in a review meeting with sponsors and key players can often work wonders. As a client told us after one such meeting: "Your candour really helped us to make progress."

Consultants can also find their position being abused. For example, some people may try to push what are essentially management tasks (e.g. reaching uncomfortable conclusions) on to consultants in an effort to keep their own hands clean. They try to use the consultants – and internal consultants in particular – to "cover up" unpopular management decisions, e.g. by asking them to "improve the efficiency of a group" when it later transpires that the decision had already been taken to close the unit down.

5.4 "Top management are not behind the project so there is no commitment."

Regardless of what we might think of hierarchies and power structures, if top management is not on board in a change process, the consulting team will always find itself running around in circles. As a project manager once told us: "Without their support, all the enthusiasm for the project is wasted." This support should be apparent even in the initial contract negotiations and should be emphasised throughout the company at every suitable opportunity. We recommend top management coaching (strategy and team development) as one of the first activities and a fundamental architectural element in change processes. The coaching sessions can be used from the start to discuss the role and expectations of the consulting project and deal with any disparities. They also offer an ideal platform for discussing and working on problems. Setting the correct course from the beginning is extremely important: adjusting it at a later stage can be difficult.

5.5 "An unexpected crisis hits the client – facing us with unforeseeable problems."

It is important to remember that the "vicissitudes of life are life itself". Market crashes, unforeseen demands, mergers, etc. can all lead to crises in the CLS. For us, a crisis is just another pattern in the flow of time. Our process architecture establishes new communication platforms that run alongside existing organisational structures. Since these platforms are designed for talking about, reflecting upon and developing solutions to complex situations, they can also be used for discussing crisis situations. It is also interesting to examine why an organisation has no early warning system or guidelines on what to do quickly (or at least start to do) and what it can learn from a crisis. Setting up a task force to resolve the situation is often a good solution: "Without the task force, we would never have coped so well with the loss of 15 % of the workforce."

Crisis situations often result in new contact persons for the consulting team, new project goals and changes in resources. They will also always require a redefinition of the contract.

5.6 "Major power struggles are in play and our interventions lose their effect."

In our experience, there is no such thing as a change process in which the two ugly sisters "conflict" and "power struggle" do not regularly appear and try to dominate the stage. One consequence of change is a shift in power. Loss of privilege, influence, etc. causes fear and mobilises regressive, archaic forces.

In such scenarios, people often try to use consultants to further their own interests. Despite all its professionalism, maintaining good and lasting relationships to all parties in the conflict is no easy matter for a consulting team. Splitting the team can often help. For example, in the case of a power struggle between the board and the works council, assigning two colleagues to coach the board and two to the works council can prove very beneficial. In this way, both points of view are equally reflected in the consulting team and assume a new level of clarity: the team mirrors their differences. This can also lead to new ideas for possible interventions. Where power issues are concerned, theoretical concepts and an understanding of the power dynamics in organisations are of particular importance: "You don't take power, power is given to you." Knowing and understanding that this involves everyone – both those in positions of power and those without power – allows for a different approach.

Power struggles between proponents of change and supporters of the old way are particularly precarious, not least because the consultants are then usually seen as being firmly on the side of change. Of course, adopting a neutral position will also help here, but consultants must above all show appropriate respect and genuine understanding for both sides of the conflict.

A further dilemma faced by consultants arises when it turns out their main "client" (sponsor) is the source of the problem: "He has no idea how to manage! He confuses everything!" To deal with cases like this, the system's perception of the underlying system logic behind such behaviour has to be improved. This can be achieved by introducing sensitively handled feedback processes, helping people to use what they learn from them and proposing compensatory measures to fill the exposed management gap. However, it may also on occasion be necessary to simply accept that the sponsor is too weak and withdraw from the project.

5.7 "Too few resources, not enough money and too little time: checkmate!"

We are all familiar with the situation: a company needs consulting advice, but has almost no budget to pay for it and cannot (or will not) free up resources for the project or give staff the time they need to get properly involved. "Can it be done on half the budget?", "Can it be done with fewer resources or less effort?" or "Our project managers are permanently on the road. We can't afford to do without them for a whole day each month."

We then have to decide whether we want to accept such a project as it stands, take it on with reduced scope or assume a different (e.g. supervisory) role. Such decisions cannot be made without analyzing the context. Ultimately, they are also a question of our confidence in our own consulting abilities and whether we would still consider the project an enjoyable and even fun challenge.

If the general conditions and requirements have been clearly defined and tailored to suit the situation in question, we already have a good basis to build on. When the goals are clear, you can always find a way of achieving them. It is often simply a question of priorities. One possible solution is to begin with a pilot project, follow this with a progress review to discuss the results and then either define the next steps or rethink the whole project. This leaves all options open. Again, understanding what will be acceptable (or not) requires sensitivity and a strong ability to assess the situation: "If you hadn't reduced your daily rate for the first six months and cut down the planned 20 days to 15, we would never have reached an agreement. Now the benefits of the whole process are clear, and we feel we can justify the additional cost and effort involved in the next steps."

5.8 "We face 'rigid loops' and find ourselves marching time."

One of the main claims of the systemic approach is its ability to produce results even in cases where deeply rooted, rigid loops and recurring, often dysfunctional patterns – situations that cannot be addressed with other approaches – are taking their toll. If this were not the case, our approach would not necessarily be required. However, clients often see things differently and put us under pressure: "What use is your consulting process if – one year down the line – our planning processes still bear no resemblance to reality, even though we all know we need realistic planning figures to reach budget goals and avoid additional strain on our credibility with the banks?" This attitude of avoiding difficult issues and failing to plan in contingencies never changes: "We don't want to face up to reality." "Why have you not produced any results yet?"

Wherever there is doubt, it will always be the consultants who are to blame. Rigid loops are there for a reason. There is an art to understanding and patiently unravelling them. Paradox interventions are particularly useful when it comes to breaking down rigid loops (as described above).

5.9 "No argument will suffice if there is no basic understanding of the process-oriented approach."

We are regularly confronted with new clients who have no experience of systemic process consulting. They think they can change people's attitudes simply by appealing to their better judgment or that miracles can be worked in only three meetings: "Surely with all your experience this can be done more quickly and with less effort?"

Keeping your composure in situations like these can be difficult, because they confront you with concerns that neither your work nor the systemic approach are valued highly enough. Yet how can we expect people to share our level of knowledge if they have had no prior experience of this approach or opportunity to develop the sensitivity it requires? Scenarios or interventions that create space for reflection can help them to slowly build up this knowledge: short workshops followed by reflection exercises, sharing experiences with colleagues they respect in other organisations (with prior experience of the process-based approach) or simply opening themselves up to experiment. The same arguments apply here: How far are we prepared to go as consultants? How much patience and calmness do we have? Where do our limits lie? If we manage to establish and coach a steering group, internal process know-how will grow and develop automatically (cf. our "Chance" example). Deliberately talking about "how", not "what" and reflecting on the process analysis and observations helps strengthen perception categories. It is up to us to teach and pass on process know-how: "I never realised before what it actually meant to steer such processes. By designing and holding my own workshops, I have come to realise this involves far more than simply moderating. It is a subtle, difficult task."

5.10 "We cannot achieve the desired effect if we are not taken seriously."

"Not being taken seriously not only prevents us from achieving our objectives, it is also an affront to our own image of ourselves." Once we have resolved this issue, the situation will become much easier.

Whether we are taken seriously or not depends not just on the way others see and describe us, but above all on the way we see and describe ourselves. Our confidence shines through. Of course, other reasons can also play a role, for example if the consulting process was never intended to be more than an alibi in the first place. Rediscussing the contract and role expectations can often help resolve this kind of situation.

It is particularly difficult when the guiding structure – our design – is not accepted and alternative suggestions are made: "It would be better not to split into groups now." When such situations cannot be resolved calmly, the "reflecting team" often proves a useful intervention. The consulting staff reflect and comment on the situation in front of the group. This avoids the need to build in a discussion break for the consulting staff, time that would not have been available anyway. If this does not have the desired effect, the contract will have to be renegotiated. The better the working relationship consultants have with their internal contacts, e.g. the project manager and other key players, the better they can anchor themselves in the system.

Another facet of not being taken seriously lies in the consultant "connecting and relating" too well with the system. This reduces the effect of interventions, because they are perceived as offering too little irritation or "disruption".

There are a few meta rules that apply to all difficult situations:

1. The consulting team must meet regularly to build joint hypotheses, go through the loops and take the necessary time to reflect together. Working alone is always difficult. Our approach requires a minimum of two consultants assigned to any given project.
2. If this does not prove sufficient, arrange an individual or a team supervision session.
3. Never stop working on your attitude, improving your professionalism or seeking feedback.
4. It often helps to recall, write down and go through what you consider to be the basic requirements for successful systemic consulting.
5. Particular care and attention should be paid to the initial stages of the relationship to the client system. Setting up the CCS is like composing a piece of music: the basic melody is written first and then played in different variations.

Established over the years, these rules provide us with a solid set of success factors for overcoming or avoiding difficult situations. They also form the basis of the general conditions we insist upon in contractual and review meetings with clients.

6. Trends and Outlook: The Future of Systemic Organisational Development and Consulting

We began this book with an overview of the basics of systems theory as the basis of our understanding both of organisations and of systemic organisational consulting. How do we see the future for this field? What developments do we expect? To answer these questions, we will have to digress a little and take a brief look at the context that forms the setting for systemic consulting.

The notion that everything is connected to everything else (like a hanging mobile) applies not only to organisations and their relationships to their environment, but also to political, social, economic, technical and cultural circumstances. Economic, political and social developments have an enormous influence on corporate dynamics and structures (cf. Olson 2000) and thus on the way such organisations are managed and led, hence the extremely close links between economic, organisational and management theories.

As in the development of systems theory, many of the important ideas for a "new" economics and management theory also came from a group of Austrians[12], all born in Vienna around 1900 and who all later emigrated to the United States (e.g. Friedrich Hayek, 1899–1992; Fritz Machlup, 1902–1983; Joseph Schumpeter, 1883–1950; Peter Drucker[13], *1907). They, their colleagues and their followers regularly exchanged ideas with the systems theorists, with both groups providing valuable stimuli for the other's work. Between 1970 and 1995, a whole series of articles and books were published which extended the popularity of the systemic approach to economic and management theorists (cf. Hedberg 2001; Hedberg and Wolf 1981; Argyris and Schön 1978; Senge 1990; Weick 1985; Nonaka and Takeuchi 1995).

The reasons why the systemic approach is only now slowly beginning to assert itself in management practice may well lie in the fact that the world has now changed to an extent unimaginable only a few years ago. The post-modern "knowledge society" is characterised by globalisation, worldwide networking, rapid rates of change and innovation, a mobile workforce, uncertainty, a lack of market transparency, etc. Yet it is only in the last few years that the demand for explanations and solutions to these issues has become particularly vociferous. Of the many questions and problems this raises, we would like to concentrate here on just a few of the dilemmas currently facing corporate management.

6.1 Management Dilemmas

6.1.1 Short-term versus Long-term Perspectives – Sustainability

Economic systems, whether global, national or regional, are each more than a mere collection of individual, independent companies working side by side. Rather they are a complex conglomeration of all the activities that take place within a given economic space. For example, the effects of the activities of an automobile manufacturer on the other nodes in its "network" and the way their activities in turn affect the automobile manufacturer are difficult to understand and even more difficult to influence. A country's economic, transport, environmental and labour policies, energy and food industries, healthcare, social security and education systems, and so on can – directly or indirectly – have as much effect on a company's financial situation as international issues, political conflicts or natural disasters (cf. Ortner 2003a).

- This presents management with the following problem: metaphorically speaking, they are sitting in a boat they cannot really steer by themselves. Reconciling the caution and careful foresight present in the network with short and medium-term corporate interests is an almost insurmountable challenge, not just for international players.

Modern commercial companies can no longer be managed using the traditional, linear "input-output-throughput" paradigm. Business processes in extended supply chains resemble a spiral of continuous loops, whereby it is never possible to determine exactly what the consequences of a decision will be at any given point in the chain. A practical decision based on cause-and-effect relationships will often – if at all – take years to show any noticeable effects.

- This presents management with the following problem: decisions intended to have a short-term effect in a clearly defined area almost always also have unintended short and/or medium-term effects somewhere else (which is why many economists take the view that economic systems are chaotic and irrational, but definitely not rational). Keeping themselves "in the know" and retaining the necessary overview can be enormous challenges for managers.

A corporate management team might well have the task of furthering corporate interests, but in doing so they must also consider and try to reconcile the different interests of all their shareholders, partners, customers, etc. Just as companies have their own short and long-term goals and interests, so also do the other relevant players and stakeholders, and these various goals and interests may often conflict. Investors may simply be looking to make a short-term profit. They do not necessarily need to link their long-term goals of survival and growth with the longer-term survival of a particular company.

- This presents management with the difficult task of having to combine their own long-term corporate interests with those of their partners or investors. To ensure long-term and sustainable corporate performance, management may often even have to resort to so-called "lonely tragic decisions", e.g. cutting jobs and accepting the brain drain that comes with such an action.
- Finding a sensible balance between short and long-term interests and goals can also prove a challenge within the company itself, since the longer-term interests of individual employees (meaningful and satisfying work, a secure job, peer recognition, self-realisation, further education, etc.) coincide only in part with the interests of the company as a whole.

6.1.2 Steering versus Leadership

Managing a company involves a combination of steering and leadership functions. We normally associate steering with the operating of machines, e.g. automobiles or ships, whereby a precisely defined steering action causes the machine to react in a very particular fashion. Thanks to modern electronic steering technologies, we can now accurately manoeuvre mechanical systems such as space capsules even when they are millions of miles away. However, steering social or economic systems is a different matter.

A manufacturing company might be made up of a series of machines with clearly defined, fully verified, perfectly interlinked – and therefore also steerable – processes, but some of these steering and decision-making functions can still only be carried out by people. To ensure functions are performed as efficiently as possible, processes have to be defined and established, e.g. through workflows or other regulations, rules, standards and norms. In this sense, interaction between man and machine in a company can be "steered".

- However, since these "man-machine" systems then become increasingly complicated, unforeseen events can never be ruled out. Well thought out warning and remedy systems and procedures – using sophisticated, standardised feedback loops – are required to ensure operations run smoothly. This is by no means an easy task.

"Leadership" involves some people "leading the way" by "providing direction" to others. Whereas modern technologies help us bring the steering of machines under control, the situation is quite different where people are concerned. Increasingly, the key to success in the so-called knowledge age lies in having a highly qualified, innovative, creative, hard-working and motivated workforce. Management then faces the problem of how to motivate all these "complicated" people with all their different interests to work together and put corporate interests – at least in part – before their personal interests.

People almost expect the impossible of their leaders in this respect: power of persuasion and assertiveness, charisma, vision and strength of character, a focused goal-oriented approach, self-confidence, reflectiveness and thoughtfulness, openness, empathy, a sense of responsibility, consideration, caution, prudence, farsightedness and, of course, sound professional and process knowledge. Some of these qualities you either have or do not have and many can be learned or developed through experience.

But as we see it, today's managers also face another important challenge, namely the question of how to instil "meaning". There can be no doubting the fact that the "meaningfulness" of what they do is a strong motivating factor for many employees (and for "knowledge workers" in particular), assuming, of course, that they are happy with what they get in return and the environment in which they work. To a certain extent, it is also correct to say that it is up to individuals to give meaning to what they do: management cannot be expected to define and prescribe what should be meaningful for others. Nonetheless, management still play a very important role in determining whether employees see their roles in the company on the whole as meaningful or not.

- There is, however, one problem involved: the different things that are meaningful to each individual employee (e.g. interesting work, fun, peer recognition, self-realisation through training, a secure income, etc.) cannot simply be lumped together under one heading, e.g. corporate success. Identifying the common meaning that links them all and then living by that meaning is no easy task.

6.1.3 Conflict between Role/Function versus Person

This long list of requirements facing managers poses yet another dilemma. To what extent can they "personify" the difference between ideality and reality in a credible, genuine and convincing (both to themselves and to others) manner?

There are two dimensions to be considered here. The first involves the issue of compatibility between these ideal characteristics or abilities and actual individual imperfections, weaknesses, fears, mistakes, preferences and dislikes.

- It is the genuine, unfeigned ability to combine the requirements of the management role with one's own individual idiosyncrasies that constitutes a true "management personality". In this sense, our prior discussion of the meaning and function of "attitude" and mindset in systemic consulting also applies to the management function.

The second issue – a situation only too familiar to many managers – is when in doing what has to be done from a management perspective to guarantee sustained corporate survival, managers find themselves having to compromise not only their own principles and values but above all also the interests of their staff.

Such incompatibilities and "lonely tragic decisions" inevitably arise, for example, when people have to be made redundant as a consequence of restructuring programmes or rationalisation measures, or when investor pressure for results – short-term profits, increases in turnover and production – cannot be reconciled with long-term corporate goals.

- With short-term survival often at stake, these are difficult decisions to make – despite their economic necessity. But they have to be made, even if they do not open up any longer-term perspectives.

6.1.4 Finding Solutions Through Research

Thinking outside the box and studying relevant socio-economic issues and future trends are more than just academic pastimes for us, they represent the environment and the basic issues that surround our work.

These issues and trends are discussed at large in the following contexts: globalisation, integration and networking; market liberalisation; deregulation of labour markets; centralisation versus decentralisation of decision-making processes; "prosumer" growth; "lifestyle entrepreneurship"; hierarchy crisis; increase in complexity; access to knowledge; technological advance; reform of the welfare state; change in understanding of the role of the state (as a service provider).

Since we felt we needed to paint ourselves our own "picture of the situation" regarding these issues, we have begun working on our own concepts and models. Much of our recent research therefore focuses on three main areas that – in light of the challenges discussed above – we consider to be of particular relevance:

- Our research into *supervisory boards* throws light on a taboo subject, namely the essential power networks inherent in company structures and their effects on corporate management and performance (cf. Königswieser et al. 2004).
- *Job cuts* cause great shock both at an individual and a corporate level. This issue also remains a matter of great socio-political significance in all industrial societies and an important indicator of the significance of work in society. Addressing this problem requires completely new models for the future.
- *Integrating management consulting, business process consulting and systemic process consulting* poses a challenge on several counts, not only for consultants and consulting work, but above all in view of the need to combine hard facts with soft factors and translate this combination into sustainable results.

6.2 What Does This Mean for Organisational Consulting?

Where does the future lie for business process consulting and systemic process consulting? The issues and challenges facing the consulting industry and the way in which it looks set to change and develop are closely linked to developments in society, of which the economy is an important element. In this sense, organisational consulting is also the mirror for socio-economic change.

6.2.1 Clients and Consultants Form a Development Team

A tried and true principle in systemic consulting is the maintaining of an appropriate distance between the COS and the CLS, based on the justification that impartiality and neutrality are prerequisites for professional consulting. Our standpoint is that in complex organisational development projects, the COS and the CLS both need and will benefit from forming a close-knit *working community*.

We have experienced the enormous pressure to succeed that change projects place on the participants and the COS on many occasions. This pressure welds them together. Shared failures and successes are emotional experiences that both connect people and release energy. The CLS and the COS grow closer together through their shared history and the trust and bond that develop between them. We would not like to have to do without these positive emotions and experiences. Celebrating success is both rewarding and important, since pleasure is an important emotion that can compensate for many a setback and problem.

However, there is another essential element to the development of the relationship between the CLS and COS: *co-evolution*. In the CLS/COS *community* in the CLS, the COS acts under order and in the interests of company management. In longer, complex consulting projects, the sponsors and participants will ultimately take over some of the consulting or systemic intervention functions and acquire some of our know-how.

- In the course of a project, the system learns to think and act "systemically" step by step. When systems thinking is firmly established at management level, development processes become more firmly anchored in the company and the COS can withdraw. Co-evolution is the "mental" coming together of the CLS and the COS.

This *working community* also represents a place of joint learning for the COS. Since systemic interventions are only justified and make sense when they initiate processes of learning and change, the COS must also assume responsibility and, indirectly, a leadership function. In doing so, it must also learn to understand the logic behind the hard facts and integrate this into its work.

6.2.2 Professionalisation – The Integration of Business Process and Systemic Process Consulting

As discussed, we see systemic process consulting as a form of consultative intervention into the dynamics of the organisational and social internal self-life of organisations. In other words, systemic process consulting aims to steer communication and interaction processes within and between organisations and their environments, while business process consulting aims to optimise standardised business processes. Both approaches ultimately serve to increase the value-creating abilities of organisations and they are both subject to the same economic constraints such as cost pressure, time pressure, demands for excellence in implementation, quality assurance, a focus on sustainable results, etc.

For systemic process consulting, this means justifying its right to exist and proving its contribution to the value-creation chain (cf. Wimmer 2004). In situations of increased competition, reduced resources, stiffer quality requirements and increased cost pressure, this can only be achieved by providing consulting services which are not only economically efficient and targeted but also take account of the relevant value-creating business processes.

- We take the view that systemic consultants must therefore look to increase and develop the necessary knowledge of business processes. Similarly, business process consultants will also have to acquire the necessary process know-how required to implement concepts more quickly and sustainably. We feel that the future of consulting lies in the pooling of these two complementary areas of know-how.

A further, closely related aspect is the need to distribute tasks and functions between internal and external consultants. As internal consultants become increasingly qualified, many consulting functions can be assumed by members of the organisation itself. In this way, the organisation can increasingly assume responsibility for ensuring that the competences required to steer change processes are successfully developed internally.

- External consultants will therefore be used in a more conscious and targeted manner. Anchoring responsibility for process management in the organisation also affects the sustainability of change: the people affected become responsible for implementation.

In light of the above, it will come as no surprise to learn that the training and qualification requirements for systemic organisational consultants have already increased significantly and will continue to increase in the future. It is no longer sufficient just to pin on a badge saying "systemic consultant" or simply moderate communication processes.

6.2.3 Internationalisation

In recent years, we have found ourselves working more often with international companies active in global markets – not just on large-scale consulting projects but also on medium-size and smaller projects as well. This not only means that partners from different countries – with different requirements and conditions – are involved in the extended supply chains and that their relevant communication processes have to be managed, it also means that the companies themselves employ people from different countries and cultures. Whilst internal cultural diversity can be very enriching, it can also lead to problems, as many merger and takeover examples have shown. Some of the issues facing companies with subsidiaries all around the globe include the questions of independence versus centralisation or individual corporate identity versus global corporate brand. Multicultural workforces also have to face such issues as common "language", shared culture and integrative behaviour.

These developments must also be reflected in our consulting approach, and to enable this the COS must increase its international focus. This can be achieved by adding new members to the consulting staff and/or through partner networks. Such consulting networks offer the added advantages of being able to pool different competences, sharing know-how of both business and systemic processes and working together on projects as and when required.

- The challenge and opportunity this brings with it for the future of consulting lies in ensuring that all the consultants in the network have access to high quality professional systemic training that is at the same time neither uniform nor trivial. We are currently focusing a great deal of energy on addressing this challenge.

We realise that we have to live and act in a world full of assumptions and ambiguities. This applies in particular to future developments. In our experience, research, dialogue and experiment are all good ways of learning to deal with uncertainty. We often take inspiration from the following motto: “Each new journey begins with a first step.”

Notes

1. The word "approach" is used regularly in the field of psychotherapy to refer to a specific way of dealing with a practical problem grounded in a specific theoretical concept. That is why we use the term "systemic approach to consulting".
2. For a detailed description of a wide range of context-independent architectural and design examples see Königswieser and Exner (2001). Entitled "Systemic Intervention", this book in only available in German.
3. In its original meaning, "problematic" is used to describe situations of insecurity and uncertainty. We can therefore say that we live in a problematic world, since we experience it as dynamic, i.e. in a constant state of change.
4. Although the term "process" is not necessarily a key term in systemic consulting, it is used so frequently in this book – an indication of its importance – that we feel there is a need to differentiate between our use and its use in other contexts. A process (from the Latin *pro-cedere*, to proceed) can refer to a court process, but is usually used to indicate a series of actions or operations. The business processes referred to in a business context include all activities and procedures relevant to the value creation chain. Production processes also include mechanical, automated processes. Although these different processes do play a role in systemic consulting, attention here focuses primarily on the dynamics of social relationships. Consequently, the term "process" is used to refer to human communication processes in their broadest sense: changes in social relationships, organisational development, learning, etc.
5. The titles of their works give a strong indication of the subject matter of this new scientific approach, e.g. "The Logical Construction of the World" (Rudolf Carnap 1928), "Papers on a Scientific View of the World" (1929–1937) and "Unified Science" (1933–1939). See also the book by Manfred Geier (1992) on the Vienna Circle (in German).
6. "Difference" describes the situation where living beings are continually trying to delimit themselves, to remain alive and avoid being broken down by their environment. They must also interact permanently with this environment in order to survive. The difference between a system and its environment is therefore both delimitation and interaction at the same time.
7. Note the dates and the locations. We have deliberately avoided listing publications for each of the individual scientists mentioned, since their biographies and works are readily available and can easily be found through the Internet.
8. Systems theorists refer to systems as open or closed. Living systems are "open" in the respect that they communicate with their environment and develop. However, with regard to information processes, they are considered "closed".
9. Bernhard Pörksen provides insight into this issue in his series of interviews with renowned system theorists (cf. Pörksen 2001).
10. The Johari Window takes its name from the first names of its inventors, psychologists Joe Luft and Harry Ingram. This model can be used in the analysis of human interaction processes to indicate positions, patterns or areas of conflict in

group problems and identify theoretical possibilities for change. The four panes in the window divide personal awareness into four different types open, hidden, blind and unknown while the dynamics of learning and change processes are illustrated in the way each of the three other panes expand and contract proportionally in line with a change in one field.

11. The differentiation between digital and analogue communication is attributed to Watzlawick (2000). In this context, analogue means that, similar to the principles behind computer programs, "linguistic" signs are used to represent a specifically defined thing. Unlike digital code, there is a level of meaning in analogue communication media (such as symbols, allegories, metaphors, etc.) which cannot be exactly defined. It addresses the non-rational, the emotional, the unconscious. While this might help us to explain, for example, what the snake symbol represents – danger, poison, death, but also life, healing power, medicine, etc. – it is very difficult or even impossible to describe what actually goes on in a person's head or mind when they see this symbol. Furthermore, there are also culturally specific differences to be considered in this form of "gestalt perception".

12. One explanation why turn-of-the-twentieth-century Vienna proved such a hotbed of new ideas and why so many artists and intellectuals chose to make the city their home may well lie in the excitement and magnetic attraction large metropolises always seem to offer. However, there might be another reason. The collapsing Habsburg monarchy was rife with conflict and tension, and its inability to reduce or "manage" this complexity ultimately played a role in its downfall. Such an environment, with all its related experiences and awareness of the complexity of society life, would also have been extremely fertile ground for philosophising and creating "new realities". The potential analogies with organisational and corporate learning environments are very inviting.

13. By way of example, we have included just two of the many relevant publications by Peter Drucker in our list of references: "The Post-Capitalist Society" and "The Practice of Management".

References

Andersen T. (1991): The Reflecting Team: Dialogues and Dialogues About the Dialogues. New York: W. W. Norton & Company.

Argyris, C. &. Schön, D. A. (1978): Organizational learning: A theory of action perspective. Reading, Mass.: Addison-Wesley

Baecker, D. (1999): Organisation als System. Frankfurt: Suhrkamp

Bateson, G. (1972): Steps to an Ecology of Mind, Collected essays in Anthropology, Psychiatry, Evolution and Epistemology. San Francisco: Chandler

Bateson, G. (1951): Communication. The Social Matrix of Society. New York: W.W. Norton

Bateson, G. (1979): Mind and Nature: A Necessary Unity. New York: Ballantine

Bertalanffy, L. von (1976): General System Theory. Foundation, Development, Applications. New York: Braziller. (See also early works on biology and systems theory, 1928 to 1936.)

Capra, F. (2000): Die Capra-Synthese. Munich: Knaur

Drucker, P. (1993): Post-Capitalist Society. New York: HarperCollins

Drucker, P. (1954): The Practice of Management. New York: Harper & Row

Elkaim, M. (1992): If you love me, don't love me. New York: Basic Books

Foerster, H. von (2001): Wahrheit ist die Erfindung eines Lügners – Gespräche für Skeptiker: Interviews mit Bernhard Pörksen, Heidelberg: Carl-Auer-Systeme Verlag

Foerster, H. von (1984): Cybernetics of Cybernetics. Heidelberg: Carl-Auer-Systeme Verlag

Froschauer, U. & Lueger, M. (2003): Das qualitative Interview. Vienna: WUV

Geier, M. (1995): Der Wiener Kreis. Hamburg: Rowohlt

Giesen, B. (1991): Die Entdinglichung des Sozialen. Frankfurt: Suhrkamp

Gmür, M. (1993): Organisationstheorien. Entwicklungslinien – Systematik – Kritik. In: Klimecki, R. G. (Ed.): Management Forschung und Praxis, 7, Konstanz

Hedberg, B. (1981): How Organizations Learn and Unlearn. In: Nystrom, P. C. & Starbuck, W. H. (Eds.): Handbook of Organizational Design, Vol. 1. Oxford (Oxford Univ. Press), p. 3–27

Hedberg, B. & Wolff, R. (2001): Organizing, Learning, and Strategizing. From Construction to Discovery. In: Dierkes, M., Antal, A. B., Child, J. & Nonaka, I. (Eds.): Handbook of Organizational Learning and Knowledge. New York: Oxford University Press; p. 535–556

Janik, A. & Toulmin, S. (1973): Wittgenstein's Vienna. New York: Simon and Schuster

Königswieser, R. (1987): Wahrnehmungsfilter. *gdi impuls* 3: 37–44

Königswieser, R. (2000): Das Feuer von Großgruppen. In: Königswieser, R. & Keil, M. (Eds.): Das Feuer großer Gruppen. Stuttgart: Klett-Cotta, p. 30–44

Königswieser, R., Cichy, U. & Jochum, G. (2001): SIMsalabim. Veränderung ist keine Zauberei. Systemisches IntegrationsManagement. Stuttgart: Klett-Cotta

Königswieser, R. & Exner, A. (2004): Systemische Intervention. Stuttgart: Klett-Cotta; 8th Ed.

Königswieser, R. & Lutz, C. (1992): Das systemisch-evolutionäre Management. Der Horizont für Unternehmer. Vienna: Orac; 2nd Edition.

Königswieser, R., Artho, S. & Gebhardt, J. (2004): Blick in den erlauchten Kreis, Eine Studie über die Aufsichts- und Verwaltungspraxis. In: Organisations-Entwicklung, Zeitschrift für Unternehmensentwicklung und Changemanagement 1; p. 4–13

Königswieser, R. & Heintel, P. (1997): Teams als Hyperexperten im Komplexitätsmanagement. In: Ahlemeyer H. & Königswieser, R. (Eds.): Komplexität managen, Strategien, Konzepte und Fallbeispiele. Wiesbaden: Gabler Verlag,

Laing, R. D. (1961): The Self and Others. London: Tavistock

Luhmann, N. (1984): Soziale Systeme. Frankfurt: Suhrkamp

Maturana, H. R. & Varela, F. J. (1987): The Tree of Knowledge: The Biological Roots of Human Understanding. Boston: Shambhala

Nonaka, I. & Takeuchi, T. (1995): The Knowledge-Creating Company. New York: Oxford University Press

Olson, M. (2000): Power and Prosperity. New York: Basic Books

Ortner, J. (2003): Erwartungshorizonte und Erwartungslandschaften. Ein Versuch, die Werte und Sinnfrage ins Spiel zu bringen. In: Wyssusek, B. (Ed): Wissensmanagement komplex. Berlin: Erich Schmidt Verlag; p. 309–333

Ortner, J. (2003): Funktion und Struktur von Netzwerken in Kommunikationsräumen. In: Graggober, M., Ortner, J. & Sammer, M. (Eds.): Wissensnetzwerke. Wiesbaden: DUV Gabler; p. 73–111

Piaget, J. (1992): Einführung in die genetische Erkenntnistheorie. Frankfurt: Suhrkamp

Pörksen, B. (2001): Abschied vom Absoluten. Gespräche zum Konstruktivismus. Heidelberg: Carl-Auer-Systeme Verlag

Prigogine, I. & Stengers, I. (1984): Order Out of Chaos. New York: Bantam Books

Selvini-Palazzoli, M, Boscolo, S., Cecchini, G. & Prata, G. (1978): Paradoxes and counterparadoxes. New York: J. Aronson

Senge, P. (1990): The Fifth Discipline: The Art & Practice of the Learning Organization. New York: Bantam Doubleday

Vester, F. (1983): Unsere Welt – ein vernetztes Sytem. Munich: DTV

Watzlawick, P., Weakland, J. H. & Fisch, R. (1979): Lösungen. Zur Theorie und Praxis menschlichen Wandels. Berne Stuttgart Vienna: Hans Huber. p. 58–59 and p. 105

Watzlawick, P. , Beavin, J.H. & Jackson, D. (2000): Menschliche Kommunikation. Formen, Störungen, Paradoxien. Berne: Hans Huber Verlag; 10th Edition

Weick, K.E. (1979): The Social Psychology of Organizing. Reading, Mass.: Addison Wesley

Willke, H. (2000): Systemisches Wissensmanagement. Stuttgart: UTB

Willke, H. (2000): Systemtheorie. Stuttgart: UTB

Wimmer, R. (2004): Organisation und Beratung. Heidelberg: Carl-Auer-Systeme Verlag

Introduction to Part Two

The first part of this book described the systemic approach to organisational consultancy and presented a selection of some of the different scenarios and tools used in systemic intervention. This brief review concluded with a look at some of the current challenges and emerging developments in the consulting sector.

In this second part of the book, we go on to explore five of the hot spots that have an influence on organisational dynamics and are particularly relevant in a consulting context. The ways in which they can influence corporate reality are described in detail in a series of individual articles on the following topics:

- Job cutbacks and unemployment, a problem that arises in almost all re-organisation and re-structuring projects.
- The effects of specific owner logic and the question of responsible company leadership via supervisory boards.
- The role played by top management in conflicts of interest between owner representatives and company management.
- The integration of business process and systemic process consulting, i.e. how to link the *what* with the *how* to best effect.
- The importance of being able to deal with conflict, and how adopting a serene attitude to complex and often paradoxical situations can help us to benefit from such conflicts and maintain our ability to act.

Due consideration of these factors during the information-gathering and hypothesis-building steps can have a major influence on the choice of intervention strategies.

Sustainable organisational development is only possible if a clear picture has been established of the relevant stakeholders and their relationship to events within the organisation, and due consideration has been given to current areas of conflict together with future economic and social developments and the possible effect they might have on organisations and their protagonists.

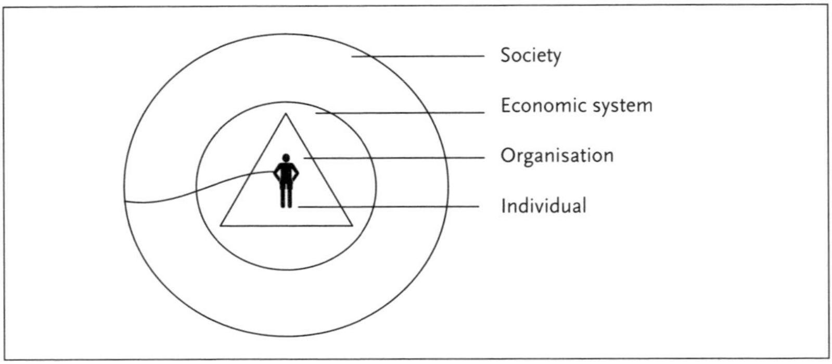

Figure 1: Mirroring Phenomena: The Large is Reflected in the Small

The topics selected describe the zones that can exist between structural power and helplessness, between the constraints and possibilities available for shaping entrepreneurial reality. These are issues that will be of interest to both managers and consultants alike.

Personnel Cutbacks
Losing your Job: Disaster or Opportunity?

By Martin Hillebrand, Johann Ortner, Lars Burmeister, Angela Krieter and Alexandra Wendorff

1. Introduction

The consulting project described in this article illustrates the systemic approach to the problems that can arise in organisations as a result of job cutbacks and rationalisation measures. But before we take a look at this example in more detail, let us first consider the problem of unemployment in general and outline some of the key issues facing the employment market.

2. Job Cutbacks: A Universal Problem

The latest OECD statistics indicate that in 2003 and 2004 around 9 % of the labour force in the EU were unemployed (cf. OECD 2004). Since the labour force constitutes approximately 60 % of the total population, this figure equates to the individual fates of around 20 million unemployed people. Unemployment at this kind of level is not just an economic and sociopolitical problem, it is also a social and cultural problem. How does a society in which social status and self-identity are defined primarily through work treat its unemployed? Conversely, if victims of unemployment are not able to see their "new-found freedom" as a time of opportunity, how do they then deal with having been "set free"? Last but not least, what effect do job cutbacks have on the rest of a company's workforce – those left behind –and their attitude to their work and management?

The issues discussed in the public debate on the causes of mass unemployment are both numerous and controversial: rising cost pressures as a result of the increased competition that comes with globalisation lead to job cuts and other rationalisation measures, e.g. the relocating of manufacturing plants to low-wage countries; new technologies and increased automation mean more and more of our manual work is now done by machines; social change, the changed status of women and role of the family in society all lead to an increase in the number of people entering the labour market. There is also widespread support for claims that the social security systems established in times of strong economic growth have created a work-shy, inflexible workforce and that existing political systems are incapable of implementing the necessary structural changes and reforms, tending instead to promise more than is economically viable.

The debate on what can actually be done to address the problem of high unemployment is equally chequered and controversial. Some of the proposals put forward include: reducing working hours to create greater equality in the distribution of available jobs; working longer hours for the same pay to improve productivity, increasing competitiveness and ultimately creating new jobs; intoducing greater flexibility in labour relations, reducing labour costs, relaxing labour protection levels and redefining their acceptable limits; increasing investments in training, lifelong learning and health issues to improve performance and unlock potential for innovation; introducing state and structural reforms to lower the taxation levels required to finance inefficient structures and reduce the tax burden on value-adding businesses.

Such arguments and formulas might well be relevant in the political debate, but they are of little real help to the victims of unemployment – those who have been laid off, those who have had to implement the layoff strategy and those left behind – in dealing with the situation.

In many cases, the people in management positions responsible for determining how to optimise cost-benefit ratios have – or at least think they have – no other option than to cut jobs to achieve short-term cost savings. When “times are difficult”, order levels are low and there is less work to go round, only “healthy” companies can afford to maintain employee levels through the lean spell and use the time, for example, to train their staff. The situation becomes particularly difficult when managers find themselves having to represent outside interests, e.g. following changes to a company’s ownership structure. The justification given for these “painful” decisions – to increase profitability and generate shareholder value –simply doesn’t hold with middle and lower level staff. They don’t just nod their heads understandingly in agreement. The logic behind their actions is different, they have their own value hierarchies and are motivated by other things. If management then starts to use buzzwords like "downsizing", "shakeouts" and "re-engineering", this not only adds to the confusion, it also gives the victims the impression they are in some way to blame for the company's "troubles".

When they find themselves unable to translate business necessities and external pressures into words and images the workforce can relate to or link the problems to issues that interest the staff, managers often opt simply to "grit their teeth and get on with it". Helplessness and bewilderment often pair up with a conscious or subconscious decision to say nothing at all. "Distancing yourself from the fears and anger of the victims and avoiding any discussion of their personal situations," as one manager put it, is not an uncommon way of dealing with one's own helplessness.

But management's refusal to communicate and fear of open dialogue in turn cause confusion, uncertainty and frustration among the staff, powerful emotions that develop into panic, desperation, fear and anger among those actually facing layoff. If management continues to shrink away from any discussion of the painful home truths and maintains its policy of silence, the remainder of the workforce will also lose confidence in them, leading to a drop in motivation levels and, ultimately, in productivity. All this, of course, is compounded by the fact that a great deal of knowledge and expertise simply walks out the door when long-serving, experienced and expensive employees have to be "let go" first to reduce costs.

A common strategy used by both employees and management alike in dealing with layoff situations is quite simply to steer clear of anyone "tarnished with the layoff brush." To help them cope with their own feelings of helplessness and guilt, people avoid communicating and instead try to banish all thought of the "problem" from their minds. They see the "nasty" change as a "steamroller" riding roughshod over their bed of delicate plants. Everyone seeks some form of "absolution": management don't want to be blamed for what has happened, while the rest of the staff hide behind arguments like "it's an unfair world" or "it was just a coincidence that I was one of those chosen".

Figure 1: Personnel Cutbacks: Often a Steamroller for Organisational Culture

This is the picture that emerged from a series of qualitative interviews we held with board members, HR managers, trade unionists and works council representatives in a range of different companies and organisations in conjunction with our research into "job cutbacks" (details on the Research Team are given at the end of this article). The interviews clearly revealed that, in situations such as this, managers seize any opportunity to hide behind rationalisation arguments, strategic decisions, social plans, staff pools, etc. Many are neither able nor willing to accept personal responsibility for communicating information and addressing the issues raised by the cutbacks.

However, sooner or later, this "strategy" of avoiding the issue, not communicating news of planned layoffs and resorting to defense mechanisms will backfire and management will find itself at odds with the workforce, This in turn will have a lasting detrimental effect on corporate culture. If however both staff and management are to remain focused on the organisation's sustained success, management will have to do something to ensure that this can actually happen, namely they will have to engage in open and convincing dialogue with everyone concerned. Dialogue with the "survivors" is particularly important, since it is they who will drive the company forward after the wave of layoffs. The way management treats those to be laid off sends a signal to the remaining staff, ultimately also intimating what it thinks of them.

3. "Facing the Future" – A Success Story

The following example of one of our consulting projects – the restructuring of the German energy company swb Erzeugung – demonstrates that things can be done differently, even when change itself has become a necessity. The solution is to involve everyone affected by the situation in a constructive, open and future-oriented dialogue.

In 1999, the company employed some 670 staff with a turnover of some € 250 million from its energy production and technical services. However, the deregulation of the electricity market had put an end to the effective monopoly status previously enjoyed by utilities companies. Gone were the days when the company had no need to court its customers, costs could be apportioned directly to prices, there was no competition to fear and staff could be guaranteed job security until they retired.

By August 2000, the company urgently needed to introduce restructuring measures to remain profitable in the face of its greatly changed circumstances. Three power-generating units had to be shut down and 185 jobs cut – up to half the workforce in some divisions. This came as a real shock for the staff, who had thought their jobs were theirs for life. Urgent measures were needed to combat the anticipated potential for conflict. But at first, the awkward subjects of "dealing with uncertainty" and "coming to terms with the cutbacks" were tossed back and forth like hot potatoes between management and the HR department. It was not until one of the company's senior executives assumed responsibility for the problem, provided the project with resources and made it his personal agenda, that the process of cultural change actually gained some momentum.

A restructuring project was introduced under the title "Facing the Future" ("Aktiv in die Zukunft"). This project included a cultural change programme and was to guide management and staff through the crisis. A decisive factor in the success of this project was the company's firm belief that difficult situations like this can only be resolved to the satisfaction of all concerned if:

- people communicate openly, treat each other with respect and value each other's opinions
- problems are seen from a holistic, systemic perspective and are addressed in an open and constructive manner, and
- the crisis is also seen as a new chance for the future.

A core element in this project was the "Action Centre" ("Dreh- und Angelpunkt") set up "by staff for staff" to coordinate the individual project phases and provide employees with a place to go if they needed information or simply wanted to talk. But this centre was far more than just a communication hub: it also organised group information and training sessions and offered people advice and support on a one-to-one basis. The "Action Centre" project team was made up of a group of well-known, respected, long-serving members of staff, available around the clock to provide help to the rest of the workforce. They listened to fears and wishes and discussed options and individual circumstances "in confidence", away from management ears. These services were available to all employees, regardless of whether they were directly affected by the cutbacks or not.

Based on the information obtained in their initial session with the "Action Centre" team, each employee was offered a customised personal development plan designed to suit their own individual needs and wishes. These coaching plans were made up of a series of different "building blocks" selected by the employees from the following options:

- **Introduction**: designed to help people find their way around the project, determine their interests, qualifications, strengths and weaknesses. The issues discussed in this session are used to draw up a personal development plan covering any training requirements or other support needed.
- **(Get to) Know your own strengths**: participants work in small groups to identify their own potential. The comprehensive, in-depth analysis helps them to determine not only their strengths, abilities, desires and possibilities, but also any weaknesses.
- **Individual counselling**: external trainers counsel individual members of staff at their own request on dealing with the situation and their particular problems.
- **Recruitment and interview training**: coaching in job application and interview skills. Topics covered range from writing CVs to interview techniques, such as how to dress and how to conduct a successful job interview.
- **Professional development**: advice on refreshing or upgrading existing qualifications in line with current labour market requirements, thereby helping people to improve their "employability".

- **(Further) education**: coaching on the different educational opportunities available, e.g. completing secondary school, vocational training or college/university courses. Intended primarily for people who have already signed a severance agreement and are considering a career change.
- **Ideas workshop**: a moderated creativity workshop offering participants a chance to run through any plans they might have for the future and test out the feasibility of new ideas, e.g. business start-ups.
- **Business start-ups:** professional support in planning a business, analyzing the market and getting started. This module is intended primarily for those considering a self-employment option. Longer-term financial support and business consulting services from the company could also be considered on a case-by-case basis.

Further options were also planned to accommodate medium and longer-term structural change. These were continually adapted to meet the changing circumstances and included flexitime work models, teleworking, outstaffing, external recruitment services and new work models.

4. What Made this Particular Project Such a Success?

In keeping with the company's existing positive attitude to corporate culture, "Facing the Future" was never intended simply as a cost-optimisation project. Apart from traditional structural change options such as part-time work and early retirement for older staff, it was also to provide the entire workforce with the tools and opportunities they needed to actively and consciously face the situation and identify their new perspectives.

The unexpectedly positive feedback from the staff and the large number of people who signed up for the individual coaching options provided a strong indication that project acceptance had far exceeded even our – already high – expectations. An important aspect here was the fact that the orientation sessions were open to the entire workforce and not just those about to lose their jobs.

A key element in the "Facing the Future" project was the assumption and attempt to ensure that no-one involved should suffer any damage to their self-image and self-esteem. Giving people this opportunity to think about their future prospects and re-orient themselves helped them to let go and begin this "new chapter in their lives". The best intentions, the most practical solutions will all be to no avail if people continue clinging to their old identities and avoid looking at things from a new perspective. The positive feedback and number of people who opted for a career change after participating in one or more of the coaching sessions were clear indications that the project had achieved this goal and made a positive difference.

A further goal of the project was to turn the company into a future-oriented, customer-oriented service provider. This kind of goal can only be achieved if everyone – from the management team to the workers on the shop floor – "works together" for positive cultural change. The fact that the "Action Centre" dialogue platform has now become an established part of company life shows that just such a change has taken place and that the workforce now has both faith in the communication abilities of its leadership and a positive view of the future (cf. Königswieser et al. 2001).

The commitment shown by the members of the project team and everyone else involved in this innovative project was subsequently rewarded. Their pride in the achievements was confirmed by the widespread public recognition that was to follow, with the "icing on the cake" being the awarding of the 2001 "Human Resources Management Prize" by the German HR magazine, *Personalwirtschaft* to our project. The concept has since been adopted by a number of other companies in a variety of sectors.

5. What Were the Success Factors?

A key contributory factor to the success of the "Facing the Future" project was company management's keen interest in finding a satisfactory solution to the problems expected to arise as a result of the planned job cuts. The board chairman showed exemplary vision: he actively supported the project team and offered additional assistance to anyone willing to take voluntary redundancy to help them start their new career on a positive note.

The staff developed customised solutions in an atmosphere of open and constructive dialogue, thus ensuring an exceptionally high level of internal acceptance for the project while at the same time providing an outlet for discussing and dispelling fears and creating new perspectives.

As time went on, the project team was able to do almost entirely without the support of the external consultants, keeping the financial costs of running the project to an absolute minimum. Ultimately, the role of the consultants was reduced to helping the core team develop the process know-how they needed to help themselves.

Having a group of respected, competent company staff on site – trusted individuals who understood the situation – working out future perspectives with their co-workers put the project team in a much better position to respond to any new developments and difficulties that might emerge.

A further key success factor was the attitude of respect and understanding adopted by the members of the core team and their efforts to look at the issues involved from many different perspectives. Although the project group often discussed fears, uncertainties and problems, it always managed to keep its focus firmly on finding solutions, not just identifying problems. The group's make-up – people in positions of influence (e.g. members of the works council), representatives of those affected (from the shop floor) and experts (initially the consulting team) – also played an important role.

6. Experiences and Lessons Learned from the Project

A dramatic change in our working environment often goes hand in hand with a dramatic change in other aspects of our lives. If we don't know what the situation will be after the change and we have no idea of the path our lives will then take, we start to worry about our livelihood and future. Change means leaving behind many of the things we are familiar with: co-workers, friends, habitat, behaviour, actions, security and, ultimately, the image we have painstakingly built up of ourselves. Any loss is painful, and coping with this pain and coming to terms with our grief consumes much of the energy we need to focus on our "new" and "different" futures. Companies need to give this loss the space it needs and should never try simply to banish it from view.

Consequently, the most important lesson learned from the "Facing the Future" project is the following: those most affected by change processes have to find a way of dealing with their emotions that enables them to quickly free up as much positive energy as possible, energy that they can then focus on facing the future. The notion that we are all – managers, workers or consultants alike – "controlled" by our emotions rather than by keeping cool and thinking rationally is by no means new, although it is something we only too often seem to forget. Unfortunately, dealing "constructively" with emotions in corporate change projects is neither a matter of course nor standard practice.

One issue in particular seems to animate almost all the organisations we have worked with: the delivery of bad or shocking news (cf. Königswieser 1985; 2003). We are regularly asked the question: "How should I as a manager, supervisor or even co-worker deal with the situation when someone is to be laid off?"

Experience confirms the hypothesis that – at an individual level – people have to go through five different phases before they are ready to re-orient themselves and work on their new identity. These phases are shock, hope of reprieve, aggression, depression and grief.

Developing a set of "rules" on how best to deliver bad news often proves advantageous:

a) Pass on information quickly and directly.
b) If necessary, repeat the information.
c) Give people time to get over the shock.
d) Don't fight aggression and depression, let them happen.
e) Don't try to belittle the event or talk about its possible advantages.
f) Don't offer help in the grieving phase until it is asked for.
g) Try to establish contact to people close to the situation.

It takes courage to be the bearer of bad news. Our own experience of suffering, maturity and ability to reflect all help us to deal with the reactions and emotions such news provokes in its victims. Being the bearer of bad news puts us under considerable emotional strain. Management have to learn to deal with situations of this kind and react in as "calm" a manner as possible. Encouraging phrases like "don't worry, everything will be all right" – no matter how well intended – will be seen as nothing more than cynicism.

In the figure below, Stephan Roth clearly illustrates the development of seven different emotional phases in a change process. Each phase assumes its own emotional "focus" and consequently its own function in the way we make the break and start over (cf. Roth 2000).

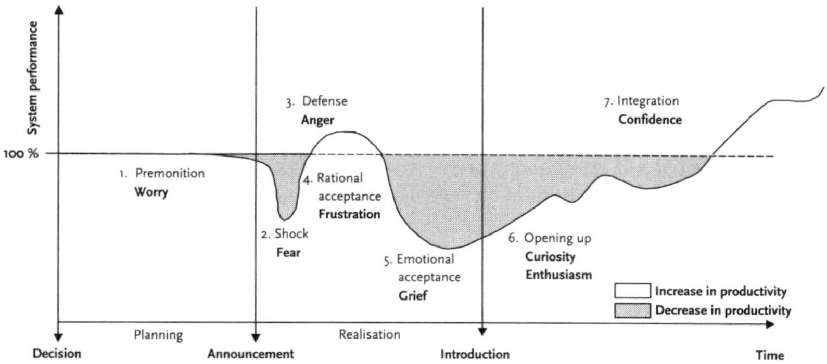

Figure 2: Phases of Emotional Energy in Change Processes According to Roth

We have developed a number of different interventions in line with this sequence of emotional phases, which have all proved successful in dealing with the corresponding emotional "landscapes". Since it is not uncommon for different people or groups of people to move through these sequential phases at varying speeds, each individual situation has to be carefully observed to identify possible and suitable forms of intervention.

Repertoire of Interventions

Premonition Phase	**Shock Phase**	**Defensive Phase**
Controlling the level of anxiety; "productive agitation"	Highlighting the situation; establishing (possible) plans for the future	Removing patterns of allocating blame; increasing the ability for self-governance
• Direct communication of facts and figures • Scenarios • Creating multipliers – activating informal communication channels • Stakeholder workshops – interviews to identify doctrines, success stories, and expected taboos related to change	• Continue direct communication, establish communication channel • Move people willing to assume responsibility into centre field • Define core issues and set up the project organisation team • Listen to and respect the ideas of as many people as possible through dialogue and large events • Remain in contact with staff even in times of uncertainty	• Publish information on the different levels of effect for all concerned • Provide information on the anticipated change process • Establish a steering and reflection system for the remainder of the process; communicate and discuss initial steps widely

Rational Acceptance Phase	Emotional Acceptance Phase	Opening Up Phase	Integration Phase
Highlighting the painful side of change	Farewell rituals and trying out the new	Broad participation and careful evaluation	Embedding and continual development
• Show respect for a former identity, contrast it with the new identity and focus on the need to move on • Reflect on the personal meaning of change – openly point out the possibilities for the future • Establish the necessary support and consulting infrastructure	• Separation and preservation rituals • Create examples and space to try out the new • Sounding boards/response groups • Point out and celebrate success • Communicate success and failure openly and actively	• Manifold possibilities for playing an active part in projects and in line functions • Trying things out/qualifications for the future • Working on corporate, departmental and individual ideas for the future	• Support for new culture with qualifications and departmental level development • Management systems that represent the new values • Demonstrate successes and best practices • Ongoing careful evaluation and focus on the future

In the course of our consulting careers, we have helped many companies deal with the downsizing process, and each time it becomes increasingly clear to us just how painful a subject this is for organisations. Every intervention – no matter how well thought out or targeted to the company's needs – becomes particularly delicate when layoffs are involved. Bringing the issue of job cutbacks and their consequences out into the open, making people "face up to it" and talk about the problem always remains a great challenge. Unfortunately, companies very often react too late – when the impact is already huge and the "surely I won't be the one" bandwagon is already well and truly rolling. But by then, valuable preparation time has already been lost.

The way a company deals with the people it is about to "let go" will ultimately characterise its culture for years to come. It has to be able to convince the "remaining workforce" of its credibility and values to be able to stride positively towards its new future.

7. References

Königswieser, R., Cichy, U. & Jochum, G. (2001): SIMsalabim. Veränderung ist keine Zauberei. Systemisches IntegrationsManagement. Stuttgart: Klett-Cotta

Königswieser, R. (1985): Die Auswirkungen schockierender Nachrichten: psychische Bewältigungsmechanismen und Methoden der Überbringung. *Der Betriebswirt* 1: p. 51–61.

Königswieser, R. (2003): Das Überbringen schlechter Nachrichten. In Hernsteiner, 2/2003, Vienna.

OECD (2004): OECD Employment Outlook. ISBN 92-64-10812-2.

Roth, S. (2000): Emotionen im Visier: Neue Wege des Change Managements. *Organisationsentwicklung* 2

8. Research Team

Martin Hillebrand (Project leader)	Managing Partner, Königswieser & Network
Jürgen Gebhardt	Managing Partner, Königswieser & Network
Lars Burmeister	Network Partner, Königswieser & Network
Uwe Dahl	Network Partner, Königswieser & Network
Angela Krieter	Network Partner, Königswieser & Network
Marion Perger	Network Partner, Königswieser & Network
Michael Rochow	Network Partner, Königswieser & Network
Iris Rommel	Network Partner, Königswieser & Network
Alexandra Wendorff	Network Partner, Königswieser & Network

A Look in the Illustrious Circle
A Study of Corporate Governance Practices 2003

By Roswita Königswieser, Sigrid Artho, Jürgen Gebhardt[1]

The work of corporate supervisory boards has come under heavy public criticism of late, and there are many indications that these bodies are not able to fulfil their actual functions as well as they should. This article summarises the main results of a recent research project, which takes a closer look at the latent, system-immanent aspects of corporate supervisory boards and, in particular, the way that they see themselves and the way that they think. The core propositions of the study will help to increase awareness of the system logic of supervisory boards. Such awareness leads to changes throughout the organisation and, in the longer term, to a step forward in the quest for more efficient, value-creating behavioural and organisational patterns in supervisory boards.

In the days just prior to a meeting of the supervisory board, companies find themselves paralyzed by hectic preparations, which tie the management board up to such an extent that they have little or no time for anything else. After the event, everyone relaxes a little, but then the rumours start to circulate. Observers and staff keep their feelings to themselves, a mixture of admiration, fear, awe and envy right through to anger, criticism, contempt and powerlessness. The members of the supervisory board are obviously proud to belong to this select group, yet, at the same time, maintain careful distance and sometimes even give an –albeit unadmitted – impression of perhaps being slightly out of their depth.

We are all familiar with this situation, and it repeats itself time and time again. So what really does go on behind those thick boardroom doors? Why are these meetings the subject of so much speculation?

---

1 First published in German in 2004 in *OrganisationsEntwicklung, Zeitschrift für Unternehmensentwicklung und Changemanagement 1/2004*, pages 4–13.

1. Research Focus

When consultants work with management boards and CEOs, the relationship their clients have to their supervisory boards is not only an important issue, it can also be a major taboo.

As consultants for complex, integrated change processes with personal experience of supervisory board membership, we felt a need to examine the logic, management principles and patterns of thought inherent in these bodies. Our interest in this subject was twofold: firstly, we were seeking to gain a better understanding of corporate management as a whole and, secondly, we were aware of the relevance of the way supervisory boards see themselves, their role and their actions in society.

The study was carried out in Austria, Germany and Switzerland. The terms "supervisory board" and "management board" used throughout the article refer to the two-tier system of corporate governance in place in these three countries[2].

However, the focus of the present study lies not on the decisions the boards make, but on the analysis and interpretation of the way they communicate and think and the role played by any existing structural conditions or constraints.

We wanted to gain a better understanding of relationship dynamics in these bodies and identify critical factors for success. We, of course, were also hoping to identify potential for improvement and possibly even intervention points to help supervisory boards address the vocal public criticism of their practices and change the way they work.

2. Research Methodology

Around 40 two-hour, in-depth, open question interviews were held with supervisory board chairmen and members (employer and employee representatives) and senior executives of large and medium-sized companies. Those interviewed had an average age of 53 and had served on the board for seven years.

2 "Aufsichtsratssitzung" and "Vorstände" in Germany and Austria; "Verwaltungsratssitzung" and "Geschäftsleitungsmitglieder" in Switzerland.

We were very familiar with this qualitative method of social research, since we had participated in its development (cf. Froschauer and Lueger 2003), and it forms an integral part of our normal consulting process.

A systematic analysis of the interview transcripts provided us with a differentiated, qualitative picture of the situation. It corresponded on the one hand to the way the participants saw themselves and – one of the key strengths of this method – also included the latent dimensions, i.e. the things that can only be read "between the lines". At the same time, it also enabled us to conduct a fascinating comparison of our own preconceptions with those that emerged during the process of interpreting the results.

The research was split into three steps:

1. Individual interviews and evaluation of results in each of the three countries (Austria, Germany, Switzerland). Comparison and consolidation of results in a joint evaluation process.
2. One-day workshop with supervisory board members: presentation of the results of the evaluation, feedback from participants, dialogue. Subsequent incorporation of discussion results into the system diagnosis. This approach has strong links to action research traditions.
3. Personal, one-to-one meetings with supervisory board members to discuss our basic propositions in an "intimate and protected environment" and obtain further feedback. Incorporation of the results of these interviews into the research.

3. Some General Observations

We called our study "A Look in the Illustrious Circle", because our analysis of the latent system dynamics of supervisory boards revealed that their structures and behavioural patterns show parallels to those found in aristocratic circles. This title reflects – and this is one of the results of the research – a behavioural pattern typical of aristocratic circles, namely the fact that whilst they might on occasion permit outsiders to take a look through the castle doors, they will rarely, if ever, grant them access to their ranks.

Although supervisory boards do not strictly form a system in the narrower meaning of the term, they can nonetheless be described as a "class" or grouping with distinct characteristics. There are huge differences, however, between the way employer representatives and employee representatives see themselves and their role. Employee representatives have a deeper understanding of the company and are in a better position to recognise the advantages or disadvantages of any decisions made.

A clear difference can also be seen between multinational corporations, large companies and smaller companies, although the underlying basic patterns of dynamics remain the same.

The differences between the three countries (Austria, Germany and Switzerland) turned out to be less significant than initially anticipated, although supervisory boards in each of these countries assume different roles and the right of co-determination accorded to the works council in Germany, for example, is a relevant factor. At the manifest level, observers and critics agree on what needs to be improved to increase the efficiency of corporate governance bodies, citing their main shortcomings as:

- Insufficient use is made of available potential to make an active, relevant contribution. In many companies, there are few, if any, expert committees or panels. As a result, work is rarely shared or delegated to individuals or experts. This, of course, affects the quality of the work, and available potential is not put to best use.
- The way information is collected and processed is also unsatisfactory. Supervisory boards receive their information primarily from management boards and auditors and rarely have any contact to company employees. Information preparation and reporting systems are rarely as good as they could be. Complex issues are presented either in too little or too great detail. Whichever, supervisory board members do not consider themselves well-informed. This leads to uncertainty, passivity and a feeling of being out of their depth. They do not see themselves in a position to make a clear statement on internal and external company developments. Whilst they enjoy the support of their chairmen, they also consider these individuals to be a dominating factor.
- Professionalism is hampered by the age of board members, a lack of succession planning and qualifications and the fact that a seat on the board is commonly seen as a "job on the side".

However, if all this is already clear, and supervisory board members are already experienced managers, then why have these observations not been turned into corrective action? The reasons must lie at a deeper level in the system logic. Consequently, the following assumptions and results are based primarily on what was observed at the latent level, i.e. content not formulated directly and deliberately by the interviewees.

4. Main Results

Although the image supervisory board members have of their own role has recently undergone a change – away from that of an honorary position and monitoring authority to a professional, supervisory, coaching body – this new ideal is still far removed from the images that emerged from our analysis of the latent level.

4.1 What Images Emerged of Supervisory Boards?

The more we progressed with our analysis, the clearer the picture that emerged of a self-distancing "caste", a power elite that increasingly demonstrated traits common to the nobility of old. This applied to their behaviour, the way they fashioned their relationships and their hermetic access codes. In the same way the nobility assumed court appointments in the past, today's chosen few assume seats on the board.

In the past, symbols of belonging included castles, coats of arms, strongholds, language, deportment, and, above all, the maintenance of a subtle distance to non-aristocrats to (subconsciously) perpetuate the mystique and air of distinction through elitism.

As Girtler notes, maintaining distance is a very effective strategy not simply for attributing importance to ourselves, but also for avoiding further interference. It helps protect our fragile personal sphere (cf. Girtler 2002:149).

Aristocratic distance also involves emotional control. In this way, members can show why they are so special, emphasise what it is that makes them stand out above the rest and demonstrate their positions of power, yet also protect their own personal spheres from unwanted interference. They socialise primarily in their own circles (e.g. at public gatherings, society events and weddings), thus further strengthening their network. After all, "noblesse oblige", and there is the "family" reputation to protect.

The similarities are quite striking. The genteel boardroom furnishings, symbols of power and spatial and mental distance to "outsiders". Protection of privacy, fear of denigrating the family and loyalty to their "caste" are further common characteristics.

At any rate, supervisory board members definitely help to keep themselves sacrosanct, keep internal problems secret and avoid denigrating the family name. Many of them declined to be interviewed with the question "Who recommended you?" Some of those who did agree to be interviewed asked for the tape recorder to be switched off and one board member even went as far as to claim: "No-one will tell you the truth!"

Depending on the perspective of the observer, the perceptions of supervisory boards differed greatly:

- From an employee perspective, supervisory boards are assigned a status almost approaching godliness. Gods provide protection, yet at the same time pose a threat. The inner sanctum meets behind the closed doors of the boardroom.
- From the perspective of more critical management board members, they are seen as a "necessary evil" that offers no support and could even "hinder" a company. "Companies should really be protected from these bodies."
- From the perspective of critical supervisory board members come images of a stage upon which only stars perform or a puppet theatre where only the most powerful, the "kingmakers" (i.e. the chairmen), pull the strings.

In our discussion of the results with supervisory board members (Research Step 2), the above observations produced mixed reactions:

- "Yes, you're quite right, that's how it works here... but I hadn't really realised that it applied to us until we started this discussion and I had a look at the examples and began reflecting on my own situation. It's quite amazing, I would never have believed it before."
- "It might well have been like that in the past, but nowadays things are very different."
- "It might be like that in other companies, but it's definitely not the case here."

4.2 The Role of Supervisory Boards in Society

Like their counterparts on the management boards, supervisory board members find it difficult to establish a clear understanding of their own role. After all, what is corporate success? Is it long-term, sustainable, healthy growth or short-term maximisation of profits and share prices?

There are many paradoxes to be considered here. On the one hand, the supervisory board is a company's highest administrative body, yet, at the same time, system logic prevents it from exercising this role. Instead of providing professional supervision and advice (as the German term literally suggests[3]), instead of defending the interests of the company and its role in society, there can be many reasons why supervisory board members choose to give precedence to their personal interests or those of their own companies. This behaviour has a negative impact on the reputation and standing of supervisory boards and is one reason why they have become the subject of such hefty criticism, forcing the publication of regulatory guidelines and codes of practice (such as the Swiss Code of Best Practice for Corporate Governance).

Faith in these elite bodies has been put severely to the test. There is talk of "takers", "lame duck management" and even "criminal activities". In some constellations, we even uncovered massive ambiguity: under the guise of the honorable board, company interests are ignored or even abused to suit the particular interests of individual board members. Loyalty to other members of the club is stronger than company loyalty.

All the corporate governance codices do is "put board members even more on their guard". Although there is now a strong – and often proactive – reform lobby in place demanding new professionalism and a redefinition of the role of the board, protectionist tendencies prevail. As one interviewee noted: "Corporate governance is only a first step on the road from secret society to transparency."

Board members are often seen to be defensive, distant and lacking in transparency. They look after their own privileges, protect and uphold the system. Membership comes with great status and prestige in society at large. Board members find themselves in the limelight, people look up to them, and they enjoy the adulation.

3 The German term for supervisory board, *"Aufsichtsrat"*, is made up of two components: *"Aufsicht"* meaning "supervision" and *"Rat"* meaning "advice".

However, at a deeper level, these system characteristics and their consequences cause a strong, latent feeling of unease, a guilty conscience and, despite the privileges, a slight feeling of uncertainty, of being bereft of meaning and out of your depth.

"This is a prestigious job that is frequently overrated. Apparently, you get paid lots of money for doing nothing ..."

4.3 Typical System Characteristics in Supervisory Board Practices

There is no clear definition of the role of a supervisory board. Board members find themselves confronted with contradictory expectations, such as the interests of the company and those of the people they were nominated to represent. What responsibilities do boards assume? What do corporate loyalty, providing supervision and giving advice really mean? What success factors are used to measure this role?

It is almost impossible for board members to assume responsibility for the complex tasks they face if existing conditions, constraints and structures do not change. How can a team of up to 30 board members that meets only four times a year work effectively and make joint, professional decisions?

Nor is there a clear division of roles within supervisory boards. This makes it difficult to control the work they do. Other mechanisms provide the actual steering, such as relationships to the elite or the need to belong. "Clarity, honesty and openness can be a disruptive influence. You might lose your seat on the board." In the words of Aristotle: "Anyone who puts security before freedom deserves to be a slave."

This is a rigid, self-reproducing system that makes sure things do not change and protects and maintains the status quo. Since the people who set the rules are not interested in change, are afraid of losing power, shy away from criticism and use their personal relationships to select new members they feel they can work with, the system reproduces and stabilises itself. This applies both to employer and employee representatives.

There is no feedback process of learning and reflecting, either at a macro (corporate) or a micro level (after board meetings). There is little awareness of the underlying structures of individual thought and action. The same applies to compensation systems, which are rarely success or value-oriented.

However, the interpretation would be very one-sided indeed, if the supervisory board members as individuals were held solely responsible for the situation. According to the logic of system dynamics, in addition to the structure, all the other groups involved – the company, the members of the management board, the politicians and the media – have to play along as well, allow the situation to continue and profit from it.

4.4 How Do You Become a Member of this Caste?

Just like the aristocracy, members are first and foremost "born into" this class by who they are and who they know. It can almost be described as an incestuous, or at least a privileged father-adoptive son relationship. Assessment centres, i.e. professional selection procedures, are seen as totally unacceptable. "It's beneath my dignity to subject myself to such a test." Members are recruited not to fill a certain function, but on the basis of who they know. A seat on the board is a calling, not an assigned role.

The more board seats a person holds, the more feathers he has in his cap, the more distinctions, accolades and symbols of power he can display.

In addition to the central assumption that protecting the network, the relationship capital of the elite, the aristocracy, is a key factor, it is, of course, also reassuring for those nominating a board member to know that they have access to people of repute.

If they were to opt for external candidates, they would have to rely on recommendations from their own ranks or from a human resources consultant, who is not familiar enough either with corporate culture or, above all, with the company's top management team. If they opt for "big names", there is less need to explain or justify their decisions. However, this further strengthens the argument for selecting members from the elite, since they are generally known – in name at least – to the shareholders.

The business aristocracy is made up of several overlapping networks. These include industry associations, economic summits (e.g. in Baden-Baden or Davos) or regional networks. This aristocracy also attends the same society events, opera festivals or golf tournaments in the same fashionable places, such as Bayreuth, Salzburg, Kitzbühel or St. Moritz. It's the guest lists that count and determine whether an event is exclusive enough, or not. Golf has taken the place of the hunt for today's elite.

Figure 1: In the Public Spotlight

4.5 The Relationship Between Supervisory and Management Boards

Supervisory and management board members are basically cast in the same mould. Their relationship is characterised by the following:

- Supervisory and management boards are mutually dependent on each other (cf. master/slave image).
- Management boards feel they are at the mercy of the supervisory board.
- Supervisory boards face an almost irresolvable dilemma: regardless of what they do, they run the risk of it being wrong. If they assume too much (active) responsibility, they are accused of "interfering" and trying to play a far too operative role, and ultimately become a threat. If they assume too little responsibility, they are dismissed as a waste of time. Given current structures, finding a balanced solution to these contradictions is an uphill struggle.

"It is both extremely important, yet at the same time very difficult, to establish and develop a relationship of trust while maintaining an appropriate level of mutual respect between the supervisory and the management boards. When everything is going well, the members of the supervisory board sit back and relax. When things go wrong, they start asking awkward questions, and this is often perceived as a personal attack."

This necessary relationship of trust often simply does not exist. In such cases, supervisory boards have been known to take measures to bridge the gap. "The whole management board has to be present when decisions are made on key projects or investments. We also insist that the person responsible for a particular agenda item at the grassroots level attend the meeting to answer any questions."

4.6 What Goes on in Board Meetings?

On a latent level, board meetings bear a strong resemblance to theatrical performances or stage shows. The role of director or conductor is played by the chairman of the board. The theatre directors are the ones who nominate the board members, who want to push their own interests through and expect loyalty from those they nominate.

Since we are dealing with hierarchical structures rather than team structures with distributed functions, the role played by the chairman is of utmost importance. If he acts credibly in the interests of the company and seeks dialogue, this will influence all the work done by the board. "It is absolutely essential to have a strong chairman, who understands and can intervene in power games or checkmate any tacticians."

The yearning to belong to the aristocracy seems to be so strong that its members will accept almost anything. There can be no other way to explain the extent of the superficiality with which they address complex issues. Furthermore, they often have access to information about their compatriots that should never be disclosed. This creates relationships of mutual dependence.

Supervisory boards rarely work as efficient teams that put the different strengths and competences of their members to best use for the good of the company. Instead they are a collection of individuals, trying to avoid endangering their own relationship capital through disloyalty. For this reason, their "performance" often seems absurd or obstructed. The official, manifest goal of the meeting does not correspond to the latent, unofficial goals of the board members. There are many taboos. This in turn leads to individual feelings of resignation and being out of one's depth.

"The more firmly you sit in the saddle, the more running mates you have. But as soon as your running mates get the feeling that you might be heading for a fall, they become opportunists."

The principle of co-determination at an enterprise level is also a difficult issue and a taboo subject. Employer representatives are careful not to criticise the German-Austrian system of allocating seats on the supervisory board to employee representatives. However, they indicate between the lines that they feel this weakens the function of the board. They indirectly accuse their colleagues of abusing the board for issues that really concern the works council. Employee representatives, on the other hand, feel superior because they know the company better and usually identify more strongly with it. We feel these differences in interest contribute to the rituals that characterise board meetings: controversial issues are not discussed openly, but often decided in advance in small cliques.

4.7 The Psychological Structures of Supervisory Board Members

It takes a certain type of personality to live constantly in the public eye, like a film star or a prima donna. Whilst a certain narcissistic tendency is a must, these are also the kinds of people who are prepared to accept responsibility, set trends and give others security.

Uncertainty is over-compensated by constructing an inflated opinion of oneself and combining it with a tendency to exaggerate one's own importance. It is, perhaps, the fear of losing power that leads to such fantasies of grandeur, the need to put others down and the constant desire to define and be in charge of the situation.

When people are finally "called" to this role, they have made it to the elite: they belong to the aristocracy. This is something to be proud of. "Noblesse oblige." They feel gratitude, yet at the same time are fearful of making mistakes and losing their position in the illustrious circle. This controls their opinions and the positions they take.

Thinking in the common paradigm of the elite, this leads to too much importance being accorded to professional and functional matters, while soft facts are seen as just that – soft – and of lesser importance. The process level, i.e. the type of communication and the power constellation, is absorbed intuitively and dispatched to the latent level. "You have to understand that there is no escaping people trying to make a name for themselves and establishing positions of power. Our whole lives are characterised by such territorial battles." Under this argument, making a name for oneself and establishing a position of power are not the result of conscious perception and reflection. However, on the pre-conscious level, this construction of reality causes stress, helplessness and excessive demands.

Figure 2: Knighting a New Supervisory Board Member

4.8 Do Board Members Themselves See a Need for Additional Qualifications?

In light of the propositions above, it will come as no surprise that supervisory board members see no need for additional qualifications. Although there is some mention of the need for professional skills and competences, there is also a differentiation here between hard and soft factors. There is no awareness of the need for social skills, competences and procedural qualifications. We encountered the attitude that the elite have no need to learn – they are already noble enough. In the event that they would be prepared to do so, trainers would have to be hand-picked, the "noblest of the noble". They would also have to be men, since supervisory boards are predominantly a male caste. "Women do not really feel at ease in the current structures and are therefore not always able to perform to the best of their abilities."

4.9 What Are the Core Contradictions Facing Board Members?

We have to differentiate here between employer and employee representatives.

Contradictions Facing Employer Representatives:

- Company interests vs. interests of those they represent (conflict of loyalties)
- Clear responsibility for the company vs. vagabond responsibility (patrons, press, company)
- Expectations on their role as highest supervisory body (everything is possible) vs. structural constraints (even good board members can achieve little)
- Assigned power vs. subjective feeling of powerlessness, being out of their depth
- Aspiration to be a decision-making body vs. practical reality of an executing body (decisions are made in advance).

Contradictions Facing Employee Representatives:

- General good of the company vs. interests of the employees
- Loyalty to the trade union vs. corporate interests, works council/ political interests
- Expected competence vs. personal feeling of being out of depth.

4.10 The Ideal Profile of a Board Member?

The idea behind this study was not to carry out a comparison of the monistic (management and control functions in one single body) and the dualistic (separate management and supervisory boards) systems. In practice, both models seem to be converging.

What interested us far more were the ideal characteristics supervisory board members would assign to themselves. One interviewee described this role as that of "a harbour pilot, previously a captain, who can guide the ship safely into port – through advice and supervision."

From the point of view of supervisory and management boards, the ideal board member would have:

- experience of corporate management
- professional expertise, generalist
- enough time

- personal independence (economic and moral)
- a mature personality, who doesn't want play the better management board member
- credibility
- an ability to integrate, a good communicator
- consistency
- social skills and competences, i.e. ability to resolve conflicts, moderate teams and deal with contradictory situations
- sensibility.

"The chairman of the board is like a conductor with nothing more than a baton. He has to know the music, the goal of the performance and the members of the orchestra. He has to position his musicians in the right place to enable them to play in tune at the appropriate volume to the right audience... A healthy portion of modesty would also not be out of place."

5. Where Did We Identify Impetus for/ Barriers to Change?

The conclusions we have reached so far clearly indicate that any impetus for change is unlikely to come from the actual caste members themselves: change will have to be initiated from the outside. This will only happen in response to strong public pressure or if the risks of liability increase. Such change will require more professional organisation, the introduction of assessment centres, greater transparency and a return to the original meaning of stock corporation law.

The following is a summary of the main points presented so far:

- Our analysis clearly shows that structural factors (the size of the board, frequency of meetings and information processes) are the main barrier to radical change.
- The "caste system" is self-stabilizing: recruiting processes reproduce existing patterns and everyone plays along.
- The culture of communication and, above all, the absence of any feedback processes, present an enormous barrier to change.
- The personalities of the board members are a further contributing factor. As people, they tend to be complacent. Narcissistic, selective perception impedes their ability for self-criticism and pre-

vents them from recognizing their own shortcomings. Any uncertainty or feeling of being out of their depth are negated or even completely turned around and "over-compensated".

6. Conclusion

The issues discussed above under the title of "corporate governance" affect the general economic framework as a whole. They call upon individual companies and persons to act. Corporate governance represents the standards and values that make up what we refer to as corporate structure. But it should also ensure that these are implemented and can thus be seen as a kind of corporate constitution.

An in-depth analysis of existing corporate governance codices (e.g. in Germany and Switzerland) would seem to indicate that these documents have no power of compulsion and radiate little positive energy for change. There can be no doubt that reform and a process of professionalisation are needed to regain public trust in the capital markets and in the corporations as sub-systems of society.

At the manifest level, there is widespread consensus on what constitutes the critical success factors and where the potential for improvement lies. However, "We seem to be under the great illusion that all the talk of professionalisation will actually bring about a change for the better. But the core problems still remain the same."

Clear recommendations for change can be made both in terms of content and at the process level:

1. Professionalise selection procedures
2. Change structural requirements/constraints:
   - smaller boards to better suit company size
   - maximum number of board seats per person
   - chairmanship as full-time job
   - more than four meetings a year
3. Organise the board more efficiently, introduce efficient work processes:
   - Create special committees, distribute or delegate functions
   - Use all available potential through delegation or other forms of communication (e.g. video conferencing), dialogue and transparent decision-making processes
   - Use external resources

- More professional information preparation, high-quality reporting procedures
- Introduce feedback processes
- Performance-related compensation

4. Hold group retreats for the entire supervisory board:
   - Corporate goals and strategies, role of supervisory board
   - Relationship between supervisory and management board; joint understanding of how best to work together to manage the company
   - Develop greater identification with the company and clarity of roles in the minds of the participants
5. Coaching for supervisory board members
6. Dialogue platforms:
   - Exchange of experience on best practices, discussion of issues for the future
   - Involvement of stakeholders for joint, subject-oriented discussions.

If it is true that with increased competition, resource management assumes the highest priority for top level management, then the issues at hand will be maximisation and encouragement of employee potential, talent pools, modern management and organisational structures and uncovering latent knowledge resources. In other words, areas that concern human resource and organisational development. However, neither analysis nor appeals for support will be of any help if the people involved are not prepared to radically change their views and break with tradition. We are dealing here with deep-seated power dynamics, core values, thought patterns and internalised images of people, organisations and development processes. Not even public pressure and the threat of increased liability can cause a change in behaviour. In our opinion, above all this involves the setting in motion of conscious processes not only for supervisory board members, but for everyone else who is involved, contributes to and supports the system (e.g. the management board, public, media and politicians).

Through our analysis, related publications and discussion fora, we are looking to contribute to creating greater awareness of the dynamics of the system. This, in turn, could bring new life into the system and allow it to take an active step forward.

7. Summary of the Core Propositions

1. The expectations (ideal profile) and reality (actual practices) of the work of supervisory boards lie at opposite poles: Loyalty and work in the interests of the company compete with loyalty and a need to represent the interests of those who nominated them.
2. Supervisory board members form a tight, hermetically sealed elite power group, a new aristocracy to replace the nobility of former times.
3. Issues such as relationships, maintaining a careful distance, loyalty to one's own class or sealing oneself off characterise membership of this elite group.
4. Many of the system characteristics prevent a professional approach, such as lack of clarity of individual roles, size of the board, frequency of meetings or lack of feedback processes and self-evaluation.
5. Board meetings resemble the stage on which an absurd play is performed. The theatre directors are the ones who nominate the board members. The director of the play is the chairman of the board.
6. The psychological structure of supervisory boards is characterised by narcissism, delusions of grandeur and the need to be in the limelight. Yet at the same time, board members often feel out of their depth and bereft of meaning. All that really matters is to belong to the elite circle.
7. The supervisory board class system is self-reproducing and self-stabilizing: recruiting processes follow the rules of relationship capital and the expectation that members will never allow the "family name" to be denigrated.
8. Since the basic patterns identified ensure that change does not happen (nobility remains nobility), the proponents of change have formed a lobby to campaign for new professionalisation (assessment centres, etc.) and modernisation.
9. There are leverage points from which change and development could be initiated, such as:
   - a professionalisation of the selection process
   - smaller boards, adapted to suit the size of the company
   - a maximum number of board seats per person
   - chairmanship as full-time position

- more effective decision-making and work processes
- the introduction of feedback processes, teamwork, self-evaluation and performance-related compensation
- the provision of training and coaching (both hard and soft skills)
- dialogue platforms.

10. In addition to these structural factors, more must be done to raise awareness of the situation and the need for change among all concerned.

8. References

Deloitte Consulting: Aufsichtsratspraxis in Deutschland. Aktueller Stand und zukünftige Herausforderung. Study 2002.

Economiesuisse: Swiss Code of Best Practice for Corporate Governance. July 2002. http:// www.economiesuisse.ch

Felton, R. F. & Watson, M. (2002): Change across the board. *McKinsey Quarterly* 4: 31–45. (Presents a seven point programme for reform.)

Froschauer, U. & Lueger, M. (2003): Das qualitative Interview. Vienna: WUV-Universitätsverlag.

Girtler, R. (2002): Die feinen Leute. Von der vornehmen Art durchs Leben zu gehen. Vienna, Cologne, Weimar: Böhlau Verlag.

Kaden, W. (2003): Der deutsche Weg. *Managermagazin* 4: 86–90.

KPMG Switzerland; Institut für Accounting, Controlling und Auditing der Universität St. Gallen: Corporate Governance in der Schweiz Verwaltungsrat zwischen Verantwortung und Haftung. In: KPMG, Kommunikation & Marketing. 1. Auflage 11/2001.

Löhrer, G. (2003): Die besten Verwaltungsräte Wächter über Geld und gute Sitten. *Bilanz*, July: 89–99.

Malik, F. (2002): Die neue Corporate Governance. 3. Auflage. Frankfurt: Frankfurter Allgemeine Buch.

Montgomery, C.A. & Kaufman, R. (2003): The Board's Missing Link. *Harvard Business Review*, March: 86–93.

Müller, R., Lipp, L. & Plüss, A. (1999): Der Verwaltungsrat. Ein Handbuch für die Praxis. 2. Edition. Zurich: Schulthess Polygraphischer Verlag.

Neue Zürcher Zeitung: Sonderbeilage Corporate Governance, 10 June 2003, No. 131, p. B1-B13.

Nonnenmacher, R. (2003): Aufsichtsrat: Beruf oder Berufung? In: KPMG (Ed.): editValue, Heft 1/2003, p. 8–9.

SBR Student Business Review: Corporate Governance, Fall 2002.

Smend, A. (2003): Pressemitteilungen Deutsche Agentur für Aufsichtsräte. http://www.aufsichtsrats-agentur.de/Clippings.shtml. Updated: 18.11.2003.

Volkart, R. & Cocca, T. C. (2003): Der Aktionär im Zentrum des Interesses. *Neue Zürcher Zeitung*, 28/ 29 June 2003, No. 147

Von der Crone, H. C., Weber, R. H., Zäch, R., Zobl, D. (Ed.) (2003): Neuere Tendenzen im Gesellschaftsrecht. Festschrift für Prof. P. Forstmoser. Zurich, Basel, Geneva: Schulthess Juristische Medien AG.

9. Research Team

Roswita Königswieser (PM Austria), Königswieser & Network, Vienna
Sigrid Artho (PM Switzerland), Digma Management Consulting, Zurich
Jürgen Gebhardt (PM Germany), Königswieser & Network, Munich
Eveline Trümpy, lic.iur., Zurich
Erik Lang, lic.rer.publ., Zurich
Ebrû Sonuç, Königswieser & Network, Vienna
Marlene Dikany-Lehner, Limak International Management Academy, Linz
Marion Perger, Management and Organisational Development, Bonn
Hardy Dlugosch, Deutscher Herold – IT Management Bonndata, Bonn

Team Players Despite Those Ejector Seats?
Executive Coaching at Individual and Team Level

By Roswita Königswieser and Jürgen Gebhardt[1]

1. Why Are We Writing This Article?

Roswita Königswieser and Jürgen Gebhardt:

Some years ago, Jürgen Gebhardt was Board Member for Production and Logistics at Audi, a VW Group company. He was also the client and sponsor for the consulting project described in this article.

At the time of the project, we both looked at the coaching process from different perspectives. Today we are two of four partners in our own consulting firm, Königswieser & Network, with around 100 associated network partners.

Reflecting on this project and replaying it in our minds proved to be an interesting and useful experience, particularly in light of the fact that we are now both consultants and often find ourselves coaching clients with similar process problems.

2. The Situation Prior to the Project

Jürgen Gebhardt:

I still recall the situation clearly: Audi was – and still is – a fascinating and dynamic company that manufactures premium automobiles. Part of the VW Group, its internal relationships and dependencies were both numerous and intricate, and the situation had intensified since the former chairman of the Audi board moved into the driving seat at VW.

The company was firmly focused on automobile development and production. It was very proud of and identified strongly with its high-quality products. At that time, its A8 model – the first aluminium-bodied luxury saloon – was just entering the launch phase.

---

1 First published in German in: K. Martens-Schmidt (ed.) (2004): Beratungssysteme Coaching. Economia Verlag.

Corporate culture reflected the company's engineering background and relatively casual working environment. But there were also a number of things that surprised me, namely the strong feeling of dependence on the VW Group, the internal fixation on the head of the group and the fact that sales activities were handled at group level.

Earnings were down, and Audi AG found itself in the red for the first time in many years. As board members, we were all too aware of the situation. Fundamental changes were needed to put the company back on the road to success.

The board discussed at length the measures that would be needed to really change their situation. As I had been used to a different way of working in the past, I dared to ask about the corporate vision and strategy. My question was rapidly dismissed with a comment to the effect that "now" was not the time for "theoretical considerations", it was the time for "pragmatic action"!

But we nonetheless shared one unspoken fear: we were all familiar with the group's hire-and-fire policy and we all knew that it applied to us – the five members of the board – in particular. Loyalty was a rare commodity, and the fact that we were all essentially dependent on the group head for our positions, i.e. our seats on the board, did nothing to improve the situation. We neither trusted each other, nor did we speak openly about our reasons for this lack of trust. Internal competition robbed us of much of the energy that should have been spent dealing with the pending changes.

3. The Brief

At one board meeting, we finally discussed the possibility of calling in external support to help address the situation.

Roswita Königswieser:

The chairman of the board felt the pressure most and it was he who contacted us through the Organisational Development (OD) department. The head of OD had already read about my work and had heard me talk at systemic symposiums in Zurich and Heidelberg.

After two preliminary meetings with the OD team, an introductory meeting was finally arranged with the chairman in his office. During this meeting, he mentioned the lack of trust that existed among the members of the board, attributing it at least in part to the fact that individual members were swapped out almost at will by group management. Once we had agreed that we could quite easily envisage working together on this project, we set about defining the project architecture.

4. The Architecture – Team and Individual Coaching

The planned architecture involved a combination of individual two-hour interviews with each of the board members and group interviews with other "relevant stakeholders", i.e. 30 top level managers and key corporate players, followed by a two-day discussion workshop.

The consulting team (consisting of R. Königswieser as project leader and A. Exner) analyzed the interview material and set the date for the workshop. A final decision on any subsequent coaching requirements would not be taken until after this event.

Everything prior to the workshop basically went according to plan, with one notable exception: although they represented some of the most "relevant stakeholders", the interviews that had been planned with key corporate players were cancelled. At that stage, the board members were still concerned that people in other parts of the group might interpret their decision to call in external consultants as a sign of weakness.

5. Diagnosis and Executive Coaching Workshop

Based on the assumption that board members constantly face an ongoing conflict of interest between their own personal welfare (or even livelihood) and the need to work together as a team to steer the company in the right direction, we opted for "parallel coaching", which we felt would be the best approach for this particular case.

In my experience, top managers belong to a privileged, "power" class and have a sub-culture and identity all their own. They are the centre of attention and are admired and noticed wherever they go: in meetings, at conferences, in the media. They almost always come to symbolise or stand for the things that are associated with the company as a whole. They share this "functionalisation" (and everything – good or bad – that goes with it) with other groups, e.g. politicians and pop stars (cf. Echter 2002 p. 30-37). These are people who find it difficult to maintain a healthy balance between their levels of self-assurance on the one hand and delusions of grandeur on the other. Since they are often surrounded by "yes" men and opportunists, they are also deprived of genuine feedback and the chance to learn from listening to what others might have to say.

Jürgen Gebhardt:

A date for my "interview" with the consultants was arranged through my office. I must admit, I was both curious and sceptical about what this session would actually entail. This was a hectic period for me – I was under enormous time pressure due to the pending launch of the A8 and the untimely departure of the manager of one of our production plants.

The consultants arrived for the agreed two-hour interview. I was surprised by the nature of their questions, many of which were directed at my relationship with my colleagues, with the VW Group and even with my staff. They also addressed issues like the general situation in the company, its lack of a vision, my personal motivations and my pride in working for this company. I could literally feel my adrenaline levels rise when the focus turned to my personal situation and my opinion of group dynamics in the board: delicate issues indeed.

Nonetheless, I was suitably impressed by their rather "different" approach to interviewing and can even recall some of the questions asked to this day: "How would you describe the relationship between the Audi chairman and the chairman of the VW Group?" Or, "If they were asked, what do you think the members of the VW Group board would say about the Audi board?" "Similarly, what do you think is the staff opinion of the board?" "When you think about the current situation, is there one particular picture that comes to mind?" "What is your role?" Although this was all new (and exciting) territory for me, the atmosphere remained relaxed throughout the whole interview.

Roswita Königswieser:

In addition to individual interpersonal tensions, a further key structural issue emerged, namely the question of divided loyalty. Many board level groups share a similar problem: their level of dependence on the group powerhouse often by necessity carries more weight than their loyalty to their colleagues. The situation was no different here. Each board member felt he was literally "sitting in an ejector seat". Since they had neither the confidence in themselves as a group to develop a joint vision and strategy, nor did they talk about the situation, it was obvious that imaginations would run wild and mistrust would deepen. Nobody seemed to be aware that this was exactly the kind of situation and pattern that ultimately strengthened the group powerhouse further.

The aim of the two-day workshop was to come up with a definition of the situation that everyone agreed upon and then determine the consequences of this definition. Ultimately, this also involved establishing the identity of the group as a whole. The clear expectations and image of the board presented by the management team provided valuable impetus. Many previously taboo subjects were openly discussed and misunderstandings cleared up.

Jürgen Gebhardt:

The workshop was held in a small hotel – an informal setting that was ideal for a workshop of this kind. No external distractions were allowed. Being able to focus entirely on one issue like this was completely new to us.

We were all shocked by the image presented by the management team. They felt left to their own devices and shared our own misgivings about the group. They lamented the lack of leadership and direction and did not consider the board capable of resolving the situation. Our dependence on the VW Group was apparently so obvious that it put our own ability to act as a board into question. We were branded a "motley crew" that was unable to present a united front and, as a consequence, had no joint strategy or agenda.

Although the feedback was shattering, it also had the desired effect of jump-starting us into action. We set about analyzing the way we worked together and began talking for the first time about previously taboo subjects and mutual expectations. This would never have been possible in previous meetings. However, the team coaching provided at the workshop made everything much clearer, less random and more focused. I felt respected, yet also understood the challenge we faced.

We all agreed that we wanted to carry on working with Roswita Königswieser and her team and continue the parallel coaching sessions. I personally advocated the inclusion of individual coaching, not least because I felt it provided me with an opportunity to unload my "worries" and, at the same time, learn how to deal with these problems more effectively. In other words, the coaching helped me to develop as a person.

Roswita Königswieser:

Our concept also involved improving professionalism at both an individual and a team level. At the individual level, we sat down with each board member to discuss his personal development goals. Interestingly, one central wish emerged from these discussions: finding a more professional way of dealing with the conflicts of interest faced by all. At the team level, we began with the development of a joint understanding of leadership, rules for working together and a clear definition of roles and mutual expectations.

6. Initial Effects, Short-term Shocks and a New Brief

Jürgen Gebhardt:

We also made progress on a business level. With the ice broken and the seeds of trust planted among the board members, we began to enjoy our first successes. We took some very important decisions, including bringing forward the launch of the new model by four months to compensate for our weak market position. This decision was very popular with the workforce, and they did everything in their power to help us realise this goal.

However, our optimism was shattered by the sudden decision of the supervisory board to replace our chairman. I was horrified. Our worst fears had been confirmed, and we had been given a clear reminder of the precariousness of our situations. Those ejector seats we had talked about in the workshop were still very much a reality. We all did our best to reassure each other of our loyalty, but it was obvious that each of us saw himself as the next to go.

Roswita Königswieser:

We, of course, thought this would be the end of the project. After all, our original sponsor had now gone. However, when the new chairman was appointed from the ranks of the existing group (a highly popular choice with the workforce), the "new" board quickly surprised us by announcing that they intended to continue the process that had already been started. The whole board were now our sponsors. The planned architecture was implemented.

After a year of working together, a strong relationship of mutual trust had developed among the board members. They came to see themselves increasingly for what they were: the primary decision-making body within a strong company. Their confidence in their position in the group as a whole grew accordingly. The fixation on the group was replaced with a desire for greater independence and a willingness to take bigger risks. The next step was clear: "We need a long-term focus. We need a vision." We were also invited to participate in this vision-building process and propose an appropriate plan of action. The team coaching became part of an integrated process of change (cf. Königswieser et al. 2001).

7. Integrating Coaching Elements into the Change Process

Roswita Königswieser:

We encouraged the board to increase the number of other people involved in the change process. Two of the most important and influential groups in the management team were briefed and played a central role in the upcoming "Future-building Workshops". A planning team was set up to steer the whole process. This team quickly began its work and, with our help, prepared and presented a proposal for the project architecture at the next executive coaching workshop. The process was extended by a further year. The architecture proposed by the planning team was accepted by the board and formed the basis of the remainder of the project.

The focus of the executive coaching sessions also underwent a change: teamwork and relationships to the group were replaced by a comprehensive vision and strategy-building process, the creation of a joint identity and, ultimately, a collective emancipation process.

Jürgen Gebhardt:

After a year of individual and team coaching, the process began to show its first lasting signs of success. Cooperation between the members of the board and the management teams had improved. Most people had overcome their initial scepticism and adopted a more positive attitude to the process instead, although there were of course still considerable differences in their individual levels of acceptance, with these ranging from great scepticism to total identification.

I myself had had no prior experience with this form of consulting. But the insights I gained through working with the consultants helped me to look at many issues in a different – more holistic – way. For example, I began to pay increasing attention to context(s) and became more aware of my own role in the proceedings.

At the team level, it was reassuring to have the backing of a strong consulting team. Their respect for us and alternative ways of looking at things encouraged us to break new ground. At a corporate level, we were astounded by the effect these new communication forms and unaccustomed process architectures could obviously have.

We gradually found ourselves breaking away at all levels from our fixation on the group, and this sent a shockwave through the whole company. Our self-confidence increased.

We were indeed able to bring forward the launch of the new model by four months, and it was a total success. The company was back in the black.

Roswita Königswieser:

Embedding the parallel coaching process in the corporate development process meant that both of these processes continually spurred each other on, a fact that in turn gave further impetus to the change process in its entirety. One absolute highlight was the manager meeting in Paris with 1,200 participants. Considered a major milestone in the project, this event was to become a key accelerator for corporate development as a whole.

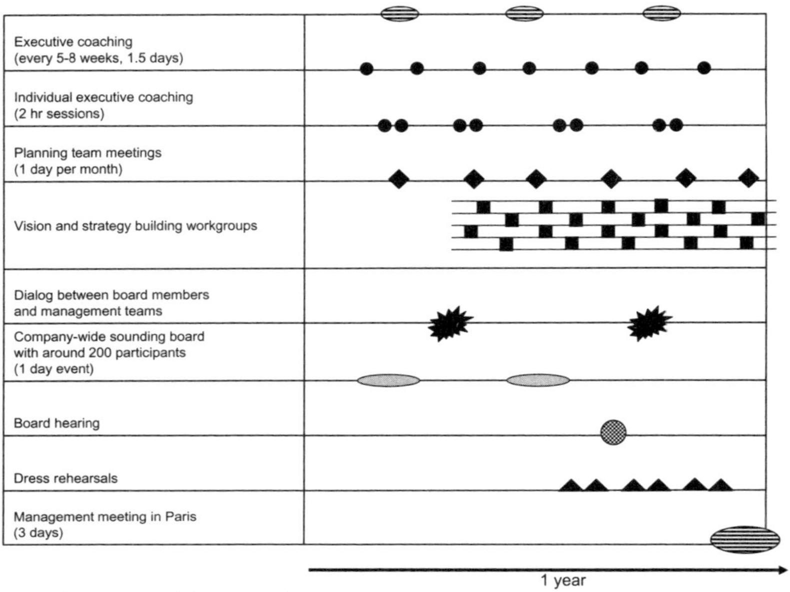

Figure 1: Architecture Elements

8. The Large Group Event as Driver and Accelerator

Jürgen Gebhardt:

The event in Paris was to be our first public appearance as a team. It was here that we would present our strategy and discuss the issues that really "touched nerves" across the company. As a result, we prepared ourselves extensively for this event both individually and in our group coaching sessions.

The content of our coaching sessions had by then completely changed. At the start of the project, necessity had focused these sessions on personal issues and on building up the trust and confidence we needed to overcome the stifling situation. Now, they focused on the direction we had agreed the company would take in the future.

This coaching had deepened our understanding of processes, and we now recognised that successful organisational development needs as broad a base as possible, i.e. it has to involve staff in large numbers – both at a management and a grassroots level.

The overall process also benefited from the fact that the chairman of the board had assumed responsibility for project management and was heading up the planning team (whose members included seven management representatives and the consulting team).

Five strategic focus areas (sales, internationalisation, etc.) were defined by the board and the 30 members of the management team. Each board member assumed responsibility for an area of strategy that "overlapped" his line responsibility and headed up the related strategy workgroup. I was responsible for "people" issues.

Roswita Königswieser:

This "role matrix organisation" was the planned outcome of one of the executive team coaching interventions. Each board member had his own view of the situation as seen from his area of responsibility. "Overlapping" their roles helped uncover conflicts of interest and ultimately facilitated the development of a deeper, common understanding of the company and its goals. Issues were tackled and resolved that required the attention of the whole team. In the past, these issues had simply been ignored – out of respect for their colleagues' work and to avoid offending each other (or so it was claimed). "The last thing I wanted to do was to rain on someone else's parade!" However, the real motivation behind this behaviour was the desire to avoid conflict and overall responsibility. They learned how to share and assume responsibility, even for areas outside their own individual domains. New thought connections were made, new insights generated and a new understanding of individual roles emerged. This was a painful learning process with numerous conflicts of its own.

Jürgen Gebhardt:

Executive coaching – both at team and individual level – played a central role in the preparations for the presentation of our new strategy at the Paris event. Our discussions with the consultants helped reduce our feelings of unease about both this key management event and the totally different approach we planned to use there for the first time. There were to be none of the usual monologues at this event; they were to be replaced instead by dialogue workshops and discussions with the board (both individually and as a group). Each and every board member would face the challenge of hosting an individual workshop and answering the questions of up to 200 managers.

As it turned out, planning the management meeting proved the perfect motor for driving the strategy process forward and gave us the opportunity to anticipate some of the more difficult issues that might be raised. We naturally wanted to be as well prepared as possible.

But, of course, it wasn't always plain sailing: impasses between the planning team members – primarily as a result of personal agendas and fears of losing influence and power as a consequence of the change process – delayed the strategy-building work. However, with the help of interventions proposed by the consulting team, these impasses were resolved, and the process regained momentum. I remember some of the more "unusual" interventions in particular: being read "fairy tales" by the consultants, taking part in "communication sculptures" and listening to each member of the group reading out the "letter from the future" they had written to the company. This was a very moving experience and revealed some of our more daring hopes and dreams. I also recall the guests we invited – customers, suppliers, development partners – and the great inspiration they gave us.

Roswita Königswieser:

The strategy-building process would never have engaged such a high gear without the "Paris" milestone. This large group event was our goal, and we needed a clear roadmap to reach it. As time passed, our work took on a new quality and our motivation grew.

The dress rehearsals brought with them some amazing ideas for the design of this event in the French capital. New design elements were created for the occasion, including the introduction of board hearings under the motto "Meet the Board – Up Close and Personal". At these (moderated) hearings, groups of around 200 participants had the opportunity to talk directly to one of the board members in an arena setting (cf. Königswieser et al. 2000). The inclusion of design elements of this kind put additional pressure on the board members to develop a strategy that they all felt comfortable with. To achieve this, they all had to speak the same language and send out a consistent basic message. The discussions in the "ivory tower" intensified, conflicts were resolved and agreements reached.

Jürgen Gebhardt:

One particularly effective preparatory event – an experience I will never forget – was the trial board hearing with 30 of our managers in a picturesque boathouse. Each board member had to take his turn on the "hot seat" and answer (highly critical) questions from the floor. We then provided each other with feedback on our individual performances. This was a great way of preparing for the larger board hearings planned for the manager conference. The boathouse setting only added to the intensity of the event.

It all proved worth it in the end: the Paris meeting was a resounding success and the crowning moment in our strategy and vision-building process. An event of this kind was a new experience for all concerned and awakened an unforeseen feeling of optimism among the participants and the board members alike. We would talk about this event for a very long time to come. It offered us an excellent opportunity to present our new, united front and set a new direction for the company. For the first time, we were seen to be working together as a real team. Our chairman in particular grew clearly in stature as the process progressed, leaving nobody in doubt of his ability – and indeed the ability of the entire board – to act.

9. Final Remarks

Jürgen Gebhardt:

During the strategy implementation phase, team and individual coaching sessions for the board were held less frequently, yet with greater dependability. This fact – and the certainty that they would include time and space to reflect on issues that would otherwise have been ignored – created a kind of safety net. This also furthered my personal development.

Roswita Königswieser and Jürgen Gebhardt:

We consider this project a particularly good example of executive group coaching because the approach chosen addresses the conflict that is almost always present in such groups between individual and team interests (cf. Katzenbach 1998).

Our experience confirms that this approach – differentiation through individual coaching –paradoxically supports the integration of the entire team. Because it is integrated into the whole organisational development process and links hard and soft factors together, it cancels out the conflict (cf. Königswieser et al. 2001). The concept tries to establish a balance of cooperation and competition among board members.

Team coaching reinforces the ability of the group to "steer the system". Individual support provides an outlet for personal fears and other feelings that cannot be expressed in the group for fear of losing face.

Goals of Team Coaching

We see coaching as a professional platform for reflecting on and resolving work-related interaction problems that ultimately empowers people to act. As often happens in projects of this kind, our goals changed as the coaching process progressed.

Initially, the main goal was to improve communication among the members of the board.

Later, we were able to address issues at deeper levels and formulate further needs, such as the development of a basic understanding for our joint task and the definition of individual and group responsibilities.

After that we were able to look to the future and begin developing a powerful and moving joint image of the company's future (vision/strategy building). Increasing professionalism in our dealings with the rest of the VW Group was a further goal.

Benefits of the Team Coaching

The advance planning of fixed "time outs" and the escape these offered from the hustle and bustle of everyday routines provided time to reflect and "slow down" and helped introduce a new level of understanding, joint reflection and development.

The departure from "normal" ways of dealing with things, the change in perspectives and the introduction to new work forms and methods provided an opportunity to move away from the "more of the same" patterns of thought and action used in the past. Analogue methods, holistic approaches and paradoxical interventions brought new, creative solutions.

Learning through feedback at different levels (individual, group, corporate) encourages self-observation, increases awareness and thus enables new, higher-level learning. This applies to personal learning, learning in sub-systems (e.g. the "executive team") and organisational learning in the entire company.

Mutual respect between coach and coachee is a further important success factor. The feedback and input of a competent, sympathetic yet independent party can represent a real learning opportunity, especially for top executives.

This kind of support and the encouragement to look more closely at and reflect on our own dark sides, shortcomings and inadequacies helps let go of old ways of thinking and behaving. New ways of perceiving and doing things become available. New ground can be broken.

Goals and Benefits of Individual Coaching

- Personal development of senior management skills (dealing with paradoxes and uncertainties, the pressure of responsibility and competition)
- Stress relief through reflection
- Pattern recognition.

Coaching Methods and Techniques (at Individual and Team Level)

In all our consulting projects, we base the selection of methods not only on our hypotheses concerning the situation and the path we have decided to follow, but also on our subjective preferences and personal experience. The methods and interventions used for individual coaching in this project were in fact very simple.

Mirroring and Feedback

- Understanding the specifics of the situation by asking questions, listening to responses, making use of "reflecting teams" and various other feedback processes.

Analogue Interventions

- Raising awareness of unspoken, latent feelings and ambivalences through questions, metaphors, images, stories, communication structures, sketches, films, etc.
- Constantly providing periods of quiet and time to concentrate, a chance to be alert, to observe and to escape from the constant pressure to be active.

What form did the interventions used for executive coaching take in this case? To answer this question, we must differentiate between the interventions used at each of the three core process levels of systemic intervention: architecture, design and tools.

Architecture

The team coaching sessions were organised as one-and-a-half-day workshops held at five-to-eight-week intervals over a twelve month period. Since they were always held at the same location, this helped to develop a real "spirit of togetherness". These sessions became known as the "tower" sessions, a reference to the type and depth of the discussions.

The individual coaching sessions that were held prior to these workshops were officially designated "preparatory meetings" because at that stage it would have been seen as a sign of weakness for a board member to indulge himself with individual coaching. However, as already mentioned, these sessions provided the board members with a personal relief valve and an opportunity to work on their own individual patterns. They also provided the consulting team with information on current issues and facilitated the development of a customised design for the workshop to follow.

Design

A range of completely different designs was developed to meet the individual issues and hypotheses raised by this project. The following are just a few examples of the designs used:

- To anticipate our own reactions, we simulated the responses we would expect to receive from some of the relevant stakeholders to an important decision (e.g. the head of the VW Group, the head of finance, our competitors, key corporate players and selected customer representatives).
- In preparation for the event in Paris, we invited critical members of the management team to a "trial" board hearing in a boathouse. Each board member had to take his turn in the "hot seat" and face the critical questions from the floor. His colleagues on the board then provided him with feedback on his performance. The different stances taken by individual board members were discussed as a group and resolved.
- To develop a set of rules for working together, we took the actual conflicts that had accompanied one of our own decision-making processes in the past, reconstructed and analyzed its "highs and lows" and tried to use this information to identify specific patterns.

Tools

The following are just a few examples of some of the tools used to encourage feedback:

- We highlighted different positions by placing them in their appropriate places along a continuum and then discussing the feedback this provoked.
- We ran through a number of appropriate different feedback loops: getting people to "gossip positively" about each other, setting up virtual customer parliaments, providing our own feedback on individual aspects or inviting "representatives" of other sub-systems to do the same. Stories were told, sketches performed and pictures drawn – all with the aim of developing insight and encouraging feedback.

The use of parallel coaching has definitely stood the test of time and has now become a permanent fixture in our consulting work. We learned a great deal from this project and, in the process, "learned to hear unheard" (see *The Sand of the Forest* on p. 96).

10. References

Bertram, M. & Weissbach, B. (1999): Team-Coaching – eine gemeinsame Gangart finden. *OrganisationsEntwicklung* 2: 51–61.

Ahlemeyer, H. W. & Schöppl, H. (2002): Ein Coaching für den Vorstand. *Harvard Businessmanager* 4: 9–18.

Königswieser, R. (2000): Das Feuer von Großgruppen. In: Königswieser, R. & Keil, M. (Eds.): Das Feuer großer Gruppen. Stuttgart: Klett-Cotta; p. 30–44.

Königswieser, R., Cichy, U., Jochum, G. (2001): SIMsalabim – Systemisches IntegrationsManagement. Stuttgart: Klett-Cotta Verlag.

Echter, D. (2002): Wie Profis Vorstände coachen. *Wirtschaft und Weiterbildung* 3: 30–37.

Hout, T. & Carter, J. (1995): Es liegt beim Firmenchef, ob der Wandel gelingt. *Harvard Businessmanager* 6: 25–34.

Katzenbach, J. (1998): Muß auf der Chefetage ein Team agieren? *Harvard Businessmanager* 3: 9–17.

Serenity

By Roswita Königswieser[1]

1. Introduction

In today's hectic world, businesspeople and managers not only have to keep up with the ever increasing speed of change, they also find themselves confronted with greater conflicts of interest and have to learn to deal with growing levels of stress and uncertainty. Successfully adopting a systemic attitude and approach to such problems requires serenity.

This article looks at some of the key aspects behind such an attitude and approach, drawing in the process on some of the emotive images and aphorisms found in the writings of Hermann Hesse.

"Knowledge can be communicated, but not wisdom. One can find it, live it, be fortified by it, do wonders through it, but one cannot communicate and teach it." (Hermann Hesse)

2. Serene or not Serene?

Some people have no room for serenity in their hectic and stressful lives. Such people are hounded by dogged determination or fixated on particular goals or things. They are wound up, plagued by anxieties and so tense that they can't let go. They are control freaks, drama queens and know-it-alls. They will never be serene.

If this is the case, is it then right to assume that the reverse is true, i.e. serenity is the ability to relax, let go, trust and be open? Some people live their lives at a calm and unhurried pace, they avoid dramatizing, do not worry about or become fixated with things and keep things in perspective. Can these people therefore be described as serene?

1 First published in German in 1990 in: R. Königswieser & C. Lutz (eds.): Das systemisch-evolutionäre Management. Vienna (Orac Verlag).

3. So What is Serenity?

The word serenity derives from the Latin *serenus* meaning peaceful, calm and tranquil. Serenity describes the state or quality of being serene, of having a disposition free from stress, emotion or anxiety. Serene people are unaffected by disturbance; they remain unruffled in the midst of turbulence, displaying a calm acceptance of the inevitable. Being serene means being able to let go (i.e. not hanging on to things) and allowing things to take their course (i.e. not blocking them).

Serenity enables us to let go of preconceived ideas of happiness, rigid goals, fixed opinions and blind fixations, yet at the same time be open to change (no matter how frightening) and the chaotic, illogical challenges of life. It describes the way we deal with our own limitations. Serenity is a form of active passivity that is hard to describe, a replacing of action with oscillation. Serene people are open, not closed, to all life has to offer or throw at them; they allow life – and all its contradictions – to permeate through them. They breathe freely, instead of choking or gasping for air.

However, people who allow everything to simply happen – or who let go of everything – also lose their true identities, so finding the appropriate balance between these opposites is very important. Only people who are steadfast yet open, established yet curious, cautious yet prepared to take risks, self-denying yet able to enjoy, can deal with conflict and vitality. They have mastered serenity.

So why is serenity so difficult to attain? Why do we constantly battle with contradiction?

We are confronted with the fact that life is full of contradictions every single day of our existence. This is an issue that both Eastern and Western philosophers alike have long been striving to understand. We find these contradictions and ambivalences in society, in organisations and in each and every one of us.

One reason why we in the West find it so difficult to be content and struggle to deal with contradictions – and indeed life itself – in a serene manner lies in the fact that our Western culture is fraught with numerous myths preventing us from doing so. The most important of these "anti-serenity" myths are as follows:

Myth #1: for something to be right, there must be no contradiction; the only choice that should be offered is an "either/or"; anything else indicates chaos and is illogical.

Myth #2: true heroes cannot be serene; they are dynamic and doggedly pursue their goals.

Myth #3: serenity is the same as self-abandonment: it indicates a state of resignation and death. Western cultures teach us to fight.

Myth #4: there has to be something wrong with someone who is basically content with his lot: discontent is the driving force behind life.

Myth #5: if we are unhappy, we have to take action to resolve the situation, find out what is at fault and regain control; everything will then once again be in order; happiness is not within us but must be sought externally.

Myth #6: everyone has a right to happiness and should try to achieve this as quickly as possible, by force if necessary: the prefix *un* in *unhappy* suggests happiness is the natural option and that unhappiness requires explanation, i.e. it is a disruption, a fault in the system.

Myth #7: time is money: we leave little time for reflection, calm and leisure, because there is always more we can do and achieve.

"Happiness is a how, not a what; a talent, not an object." (Hermann Hesse)

We can only be happy if we expect nothing from tomorrow and gratefully accept what today has to offer; the moments of magic will come back time and again." (Hermann Hesse)

These myths are an expression of a basic attitude formed historically through our belief in progress and our performance-oriented society and based on postmodern values. We do not want to go into this development in any detail here, but simply to mention some of the points that lead to these values and perceptions.

Throughout the Age of Reason, when philosophers looked upon understanding as the path to true freedom, the concepts of rational ethics, morality, virtue and duty played an important role, whereas irrational emotions, egoism and preferences were despised. Through the differentiation of the sciences and technologies and the division of labour, the holistic view gave way to linear progress. The belief in continual progress, the exaggeration of the realms of feasibility and the limits of control over nature – over what is irrational, intuitive, physical and even feminine – led to the development of a culture of self-control, discipline and singular logic and the illusion of mutually accepted objectivity.

There is no place in such an environment for serenity, wisdom, calm or tranquility.

But this old form of culturally-specific "rationality" has now reached its limits. We moan about the high price to be paid and receive a rude reminder of the limits of our powers and control in return (environmental problems, population growth, psychosomatic disorders, futility syndrome, etc.). At the same time, a paradigm change and a cultural shift is underway, as the crisis forces us to rethink these values. It can be no coincidence that Capra's *The Turning Point* (Capra 1982) has become a bestseller, people are joining Zen groups in droves, interest in Eastern philosophies and mysticism is on the increase, green movements and alternative societies are gaining in popularity, while peace and women's rights movements and citizens action groups have become strong political lobbies. This paradigm change brings the lost, holistic way of thinking back out into the open and, in the process, puts the suppressed, rejected interests back into fashion.

Serenity is not only an interesting attitude, it is also a necessary philosophy of life.

4. The Pursuit of Serenity

4.1 Accept yourself

"If you do not have a positive image of yourself, if you have not accepted yourself as a friend," said Lao Tse, *"you cannot be serene."* If you do not like yourself, you will project this image to your environment. People who are happy in themselves are happy with others. Those who can forgive themselves are also forgiving to others. As Descartes observes, *"What Peter says about Paul says more about Peter than it does about Paul."*

The environment is like a mirror image of our inner lives. We think that we are seeing reality, when in actual fact we are only seeing ourselves. The things that annoy us about other people (e.g. partners or co-workers) are generally the things we fear and reject most in ourselves.

"If you hate a person, you hate something in him that is a part of yourself. What isn't part of ourselves doesn't disturb us." (Hermann Hesse)

However, accepting ourselves does not then mean that we can sit back and rest on our laurels. Quite the reverse: we have to continue to work on ourselves and learn to accept the darker sides of our character. The notion that accepting ourselves is the key to a positive life is also found in the writings of Seneca. When approached in the year 53 AD by a fire brigade captain who could not find inner peace because he always regretted the things he had begun and feared those that were to come, the philosopher summed up the symptoms as follows:

"You are neither happy nor content in yourself. That's the cause of all your doom and gloom."

Most psychological concepts also address the self-acceptance issue. For example, the psychoanalytical process in particular assumes that non-neurotic behaviour is only possible when an analysand has accepted himself and reintegrated the things he had previously suppressed, rejected and cut out, i.e. when he no longer wants to be something he is not. We can only love others to the same extent we love ourselves. When we hug someone, we also hug ourselves. When we hit someone, we also hurt ourselves.

4.2 You Hold the Key

The Grimm's fairy tale *Hans in Luck* demonstrates that true happiness is not to be found in gold or other material objects; we have to look for it in ourselves. Happiness is not confined to the existence of one thing or another. We can simply just be happy, for no other apparent reason than that.

If we don't accept ourselves for what we are – if we have no self-respect – we will not be able to accept others for what they are either. Self-acceptance is a prerequisite for serenity.

The notion that self-affirmation is also the key to success is confirmed by Warren Bennis in his study of highly successful managers. He concludes that self-esteem has a magnetic effect on others, because it also inspires in them a feeling of self-confidence. Good managers believe both in themselves and their staff.

4.3 Develop a Positive World-View

Our view of the world, of life, people, organisations, etc. is, of course, closely linked to the image we have of ourselves. If we generally take a positive outlook on life and assume that life has a meaning, we will try to find a place for everything in this horizon of meaning. Conversely, if we see life as a burden, as a vale of tears, we will tend to see negative events as confirmation of this, while dismissing any positive aspects of life simply as brief interludes, as exceptions that prove the rule. People who take such a bleak view of the world usually see themselves as downtrodden victims. In their worlds, there are only winners and losers, perpetrators and victims, rights and wrongs, the fortunate and the unfortunate.

Serene people see the world from a different perspective. They consider life to be worth living and that there is meaning to their existence. They believe that life will find its own best path. They know there is more than one way to lead a meaningful life. They accept that they themselves hold the key to defining their own lives. They see themselves as perpetrators not victims and accept the consequences of their actions. They seek not to blame others, but rather think of what they themselves can do to improve a situation. They consider strokes of fate to be a part of life that often hide an opportunity to develop and change.

Serenity is not dependent on how many things fate actually throws in our path, but on our basic assumption of on balance how good or bad life is.

Only people who are willing to be content will actually experience contentment. Serene people don't blame circumstance or other people. They are able to make the best out of every situation because they feel responsible for their own lives. If they fail at something, they don't feel guilty, but instead assume responsibility and face up to the consequences. They know it is they who determine how good their lives will be and do not seek to push problems onto their parents, elders or even their line managers.

"The goal of wisdom is to only grant things as much power over us as we wish them to have and to no longer receive our destiny from outside, but take it in our own hands like a breath from within." (Hermann Hesse)

Serenity is given preference over bitterness. They know they cannot influence everything that might be important to them and while many things might irritate them, they see these setbacks as learning opportunities and live their lives with an attitude of carefree serenity.

"Being carefree is neither dalliance nor complacency, it is sublime awareness and love, affirmation of all realities, being vigilant at the brink of the abyss." (Hermann Hesse)

People who are serene are confident of their abilities and believe that we are born into a good world. For example, drivers who are scared of tackling a winding mountain road conjure up all manner of frightening images of the accidents and injuries that might occur. Confident drivers not only enjoy the scenic drive, they also have a clear view of the road ahead.

"Men are disturbed, not by things, but by the principles and notions which they form concerning things." (Epictetus)

Whilst we are not solely responsible for the things that happen, we are responsible for the way we interpret them, the way they affect us and what we then make of them.

Ultimately, it is all a question of our personal perception of reality. There is no objective truth, only our own interpretations of reality. We are woven into a web of meaning that is of our own making.

People with a positive outlook tend to interpret strokes of fate or worrying events differently and have other ways of describing them. For example, successful managers do not talk about setbacks or failures, they talk of learning, setting new directions or making the best of new opportunities.

However, even a positive view of the world is not without its problems. Nonetheless, these problems should not be seen as a reason to simply give up. Instead they should be recognised for what they are, i.e. new breaks, challenges and chances. When attitudes change, it is in fact not the people and events that have changed, but the way we ourselves experience the situation. For example, when struck down by ill health, we might initially feel that fate has dealt us an unfair hand. Only later do we come to recognise the important role such an illness might have played in our development. Whilst we might at one stage have chastised our parents for a loveless relationship, we later come to realise that this painful experience helped us in later life to develop greater compassion for others. At the time it might have seemed to signal the end of everything we knew, but we may later come to see divorce as the start of a new, brighter and more independent future.

The way we judge things depends on our view of the world, our self-confidence and the context we accord them. A serene person will always see both sides of the coin.

The view of the world we carry with us ultimately also colours the way we see other people (e.g. our families, friends and co-workers). If someone doesn't do something the way we want them to, we are left with two options: we either think of them as a hopeless cause or we put it down to a lack of experience. We can accuse someone of malicious intent or give them the benefit of the doubt and assume they acted in good faith. When things go wrong, we can either look for a scapegoat or simply see the problem as symptomatic of a defect in the system. Serenity helps us to see that things are the way they are, accept the consequences and learn from what has happened. Paradoxically, it is when they learn to accept the way they are that people change, not by giving in to constant pressure. To change other people, we have to start by changing ourselves and our own attitudes. This wisdom is illustrated in the following Taoist story:

Before Yen-Ho took up his duties as a teacher in the house of the Duke of Wei, he went to Chu Po Yu to ask for advice. "My new master is a cruel and bloodthirsty man," he said. "How should I treat a man like that?" "That is a good question," replied Chu Po Yu. "You must start by improving yourself, not him."

This self-fulfilling prophecy also highlights the connection between expected and actual behaviour. We don't just see what we expect to see, we also act accordingly, in line with our current expectations.

4.4 Learn to Live With Contradiction

Being serene means being open to both the positive and the negative aspects of life. This, in turn, means giving space to feelings and wishes we are ashamed of and would prefer to ignore. Everything we push away, reject or suppress leads to tension, blocked energies and other symptoms. In her book *Patterns of Childhood* (1984), Christa Wolf notes that feelings we deny will catch up with us in the end.

If we are sad – perhaps because we feel in some way rejected – we should let this grief take its course. Margarete Mitscherlich (1972) describes grief as a process that involves a gradual acceptance of loss, an experience that can help us develop and mature as a person. This includes, for example, breaking or restructuring emotional ties that have lost their relevance.

If we fall in love with someone else when we are already in another relationship, we should welcome this feeling, no matter how frightening, chaotic yet beautiful it might be. If we at times feel we hate someone we love, we should not try to repress it. If we face a completely new experience, something that threatens to overturn everything we have established up to that point – for example a change of career – we should embrace this opportunity.

Not all of these things can be positive: destructive impulses are also a part of us. Evil is an important element of reality.

"If not for the beast within us we would be castrated angels." (Hermann Hesse)

"I am often tired and without the belief and will to act, yet I believe we should not fight these emotions, but drift with them instead, at times crying, at times thoughtlessly brooding; later it will emerge that our souls have indeed gone on living, and something in us has moved on." (Hermann Hesse)

Being able to let things happen means keeping your spirit agile. Serenity enables us to accept contradictions, embrace the new and, in the process, come to terms with and harness the energy to be found in our own fears. In this sense, serenity is not – as is often claimed –turning our backs on life, an act of surrender, passivity, self-abandonment, denial or inertia, but rather a calm and constant way of dealing with ourselves and the world around us.

The Stoic Seneca asks, "*Do we human beings not have the strength to free ourselves of anything that could threaten us? All we need to do is remain indifferent or frozen to the world and not let ourselves be affected by anything that happens.*" In his epistle *On the Happy Life* he recommends we become impervious to heat, to cold and to insults, as well as to the sweet emotions that make us dependent on any form of happiness. Serenity is not a protective layer of skin or armour plating that keeps out unpleasant things, nor is it an anaesthesia of the body and soul. Happiness does not mean that we stop having needs, wishes or fears.

4.5 Let Go of Fixations

Serenity also means being able to let go. If we resolutely follow a certain path or goal, e.g. reaching a position of power, and are prepared to sacrifice other qualities in the process, we cannot be serene. If we are fixated on a particular relationship and think we will only ever be happy with that one person, we become possessive, jealous and anxious. Dialectics are especially relevant in human relationships: to really love someone, we also have to be able to let them go. Love is really nothing more than a guest. It usually only comes when it doesn't have to. We can't ask or force it to come, nor can we make it stay. Love is a child of freedom. Any attempt to contain it, control it or force a commitment will ultimately destroy it.

For example, people who are unhappy because they have too few relationships in their lives are perhaps simply trying too hard. There is a strong possibility that they do not accept others the way they are – at face value – and try instead to change them.

If we try to keep our children under our control and tie them to us, we will lose them. If we let them go, they will return as independent human beings.

To be serene, we may have to forsake some things we think are essential. These could include people, goals or convictions. The greater our self-esteem, the more we will be at peace with ourselves and the easier this becomes.

Time and again we find ourselves confronted with situations in which we cannot have what we really want or we must relinquish things we have come to love and cherish. We have to regain control of our lives after a divorce or come to terms with the death of a loved one. Serenity is particularly significant in situations of extreme loss or relinquishment. Freud refers to this letting go of things we thought we could never do without as the "work of mourning" (*Trauerarbeit*). It involves working through our anger and grief and then integrating reality into our own identity. Again, the solution here lies in a paradox: the only way out of depression is to address it head on. To deal with anger, we have to "embrace" it. People who are able to accept their feelings, admit their emotions and then work their way through them, are the ones who will ultimately also be able to move on.

Serenity also means dealing with disillusionment, taking leave of unattainable desires, loved ones, children who have grown up, colleagues who have moved on to new pastures and pipe dreams. Trying to hold on makes the "work of mourning" all the more difficult. Without feeling and accepting the suffering and disappointment, we cannot come to terms with reality. We are not trying to convince ourselves that the loss is unimportant, that the pain is not really that bad, or that the grapes would have been sour anyway. Rather we are trying to acknowledge that grief hurts, it hurts so badly that we feel it will tear us apart and we will lose all concept of reality. We must face these feelings without self-pity and without trying to rationalise them.

"You should not suppress longing, you must surrender to it." (Hermann Hesse)

The extent to which an obsessive need to hold on to something or achieve a particular goal makes other objectives impossible manifests itself in many different ways. Insomniacs who try to force themselves to sleep only make their situation worse. If they stop thinking about it, sleep often comes of its own accord.

A lonely heart who desperately seeks someone to fall in love with usually finds that the search has been in vain. We frequently encounter that "all important" person when we least expect it or may even have given up on the idea.

Being able to let go also depends strongly on our own opinions, ideas and convictions, which are in turn linked to the way we see others and ourselves.

If we do not question or let go of these ideas and convictions from time to time, we block the way for new experiences. Adhering strictly to existing convictions can severely limit our ability to embrace new things. "Convictions" are rigid, unshakable beliefs. Things that do not conform to our convictions are either ignored, dismissed or redefined. Conviction obstructs our view, prevents us from understanding other truths. Holding on to these beliefs makes us blind and opinionated, it causes us to condemn others and over-dramatise situations in which we feel we have been unjustly treated. In the process, we simply ignore the fact that we ourselves are to blame for this persecution. By forcing others to accept our version of the truth, we assume that their version is wrong and thereby provoke the resultant polarisation.

However, this does not mean that serene people have no convictions, have no standpoint or act without motivation or enthusiasm, they simply distance themselves from the notion that theirs is the one and only correct truth. Serenity means not always having to be right and, therefore, accepting that others are not always wrong. It means recognizing the relativity and subjectivity of our own opinions, being open to things that are different or strange and having the self-confidence to abandon or change established ways of thinking. Can a serene person be politically active and critical? Does the serene revolutionary actually exist? We think so, but that the types of resistance they use are different. Gandhi, for example, was a serene revolutionary who succeeded in implementing a strategy of pacifism.

Being able to let go is an essential requirement for progress. The literature on organisational innovation processes indicates that the primary challenges facing organisations are the need to confront unfamiliar, dissonant information and discard old mindsets. If there is no willingness to do so, then innovation is not possible.

4.6 Live in the Present

Many people are either so worried about what the future will hold or so preoccupied with worries from the past that they are unable to live in the present. They lament their unhappy childhoods and compare themselves with people whose futures appear to be rosier. They can list all the things they need to make them happy and contented: the right partner, a better job, more money, their youth, etc. At the other end of the spectrum, serene people accept life as it is and do not wait self-pityingly for things to change. They neither see themselves as victims, nor do they wait for the improbable to happen. They do not wait for someone else to come along and save them, they accept responsibility for their own lives and grasp the possibilities on offer. They paddle downriver with the flow of energy, instead of upstream against the current.

Because we are so busy fixating on specific things, we often don't see the beauty and opportunity all around us. The future has always already begun. Serene people feel that things are good just the way they are. Everything is in a constant state of change. We cannot hold on to the beautiful things forever. But the pain will also go away again. Living in the present means finding ourselves now. The secret of serenity lies in living for today, not waiting for tomorrow. In other words: the way is the goal! If we have faith in ourselves, we will not be constantly worried. Serenity floats on a carefree, wispy cloud.

But adopting such an attitude does not mean forgoing our visions, hopes and dreams. It means being upbeat, constantly learning and living life to the fullest in the here and now. A serene person can be compared to a Zen archer who perfects his skills to such an extent that his desire to hit the target disappears and archer, arrow and target become inseparable elements in the same process.

With serenity comes a particular attitude towards time, one in which stress and a hectic lifestyle do not play a role. This does not simply mean having time; it means taking time to relax. The present is important, because in it the past and the future are – in Hegel's sense of the word – also preserved (*aufgehoben*).

We still tend to seek an escape from stress outside our work. Perhaps shorter working hours are the answer? But this would then mean the same work has to be completed under greater time pressure. Yet dealing with stress should be the opposite of pressure, an anti-stress regime. Dealing with stress means getting rid of negative pressure while we work, concentrating on and putting all our energy into the task in hand. When we are stressed, our thoughts are permanently elsewhere, and we find ourselves constantly being torn apart. Being serene means focusing on the here and now, centring on the current situation, letting go, concentrating on what is happening now, what we are doing at the moment and what we want or have to do.

A central key to attaining this is the Zen principle "*do what you do*". In essence, this means being conscious and fully aware of everything we do.

A Zen monk was asked how he managed to remain so calm when he had so many things to do. He replied, "When I stand, I stand. When I walk, I walk. When I sit, I sit. When I eat, I eat. When I speak, I speak". When he had finished, the people said, "But that is what we do. What else do you do?" The monk repeated his previous words. Again the people said, "But that's exactly what we do." "No," he explained, "when you sit, you are already standing. When you stand, you are already running. When you run, you are already at the finish line."

All of these recommendations ultimately have an impact on each other. They are all expressions of one and the same basic approach, an approach in which our attitudes to the world and to ourselves manifest themselves. Serenity is a movement that happily resonates in time with life's contradictions and, at the same time, a stillness that rests deep within us.

5. References

Capra, F. (1982): The Turning Point: Science, Society, and the Rising Culture. New York: Simon & Schuster.

Wolf, C. (1984): Patterns of Childhood. New York: Farrar, Straus & Giroux.

Mitscherlich, M. (1972): Müssen wir hassen? Über den Konflikt zwischen innerer und äußerer Realität. Munich: Piper Verlag

An Integrated Approach to Business and Systemic Process Consulting

By Roswita Königswieser, Ebrû Sonuç and Jürgen Gebhardt[1]

1. Why Combine Business and Systemic Process Consulting?

In this article we examine the possible benefits to clients of a new business model which combines and integrates two different forms of consulting: business process and systemic process consulting. We report on our own experiences of working in this type of combined consulting setting and present the general requirements and success factors for projects of this kind, drawing in the process on conclusions and information from our own research reports.

As systemic organisational developers or systemic process consultants (we use the terms synonymously) we regularly encounter the limits of compatibility of business and systemic process consulting, be it in restructuring projects, in mergers or with the introduction of new production systems. Splitting things up into hard and soft factors, into content and processes is common practice in the traditional Western view of the world with its mechanistic paradigms, whereas the holistic view taken by the systemic approach focuses basically on integrating contradictory positions and extremes (see section 2).

For many years this differentiation also proved useful in determining the various areas of expertise, assigning roles and setting the boundaries between the individual consulting firms and services available. Even clients seemed to find it easy to distinguish between the two consulting approaches, basing their choice on the following simple maxim: "If we need to increase our production levels, we call in business process consultants; if we want to change our corporate culture, then it's systemic consultancy we need."

In the meantime, many clients and consultants (regardless of approach) have come to the conclusion that this division of roles is nei-

1 First published in German in: M. Mohe (ed.) (2005): In the Neighbourhood of Consulting. Neue Geschäftsmodelle im Beratungsmarkt. Leonberg (Rosenberger Fachverlag).

ther effective nor desirable. Indeed, as former McKinsey associates Tom Peters and Robert Waterman note in their bestseller (cf. Peters and Waterman 1982), organisations achieve the best results when they consider a combination of hard factors ("strategies, structures, systems") and soft factors ("staffing, skills, shared values, style of management").

But theory is one thing and practice another. The lack of a common view shared by managers and consultants alike continues to bring about this split into business and systemic process consulting. This, in turn, can lead to a situation where two different consulting firms with their two different approaches and areas of expertise are hired at the same time by the same company. The arduous task of pulling together the loose, unconnected threads is often left simply to chance, and the results are by no means satisfactory for the client since each firm ultimately bases any proposed solutions on its own particular approach and consulting focus, leaving the client confused by the range and number of different recommendations.

Situations like this only serve to highlight the need for support from the consulting sector itself in bringing together the different approaches, resources and fields of expertise, thereby providing a new level of impetus to consulting and fostering organisational development.

2. Integration Problems – The Main Differences between the Two Approaches

Juxtaposing the ways the two approaches consider themselves provides a strong indication of where the integration problems might lie. Critics of a business process-oriented approach speak of "extended workbenches" for top management, "selling pseudo-collateral" or "know-it-all consultants" (Zech 2004). Yet from the business process consultants' own perspective, it is precisely because they do "know better" that they don't suffer from "corporate tunnel vision" and they can offer better, more neutral solutions and new ways of solving problems that they are approached in the first place.

Disparagers of systemic process consulting brand it as "on the fence" moderation by "softies" or "fair weather consultants" who "block out the business side of the situation". But this doesn't worry the process consultants; they see themselves as coaches and guides on a learning journey and consider their role as one of "changing patterns" and "empowering" people with new skills for the future.

Attempts to establish a neutral, shared definition uncover a number of fundamental differences between the two approaches.

The term *business process consulting* is used to refer to those consulting services in which specially trained consultants use their expertise in such fields as business studies, engineering, etc. to help companies solve specific business problems. In their consulting activities, they draw primarily on standardised knowledge and their own skills in interpreting the data available.

They see these data as problem indicators and use them to identify the reasons behind a specific issue. In this approach, the solution then lies in the proper and accurate selection, linking and interpretation of the data. The logic behind the interpretation and the resultant options it uncovers corresponds to a more or less complicated, complex, yet "rational" cause-effect pattern; a pattern to which social processes have to adapt and comply. The focus of attention lies on function-specific logic, e.g. the logic behind production, purchasing or sales.

This very particular function-specific view of the logic behind processes and structures has far-reaching consequences for consulting practice. Although experienced business consultants do make some use of the tools and techniques available for steering social processes in their assessment of the actual situation and recommendations for achieving the target situation, communication and social interaction do not play a central role in their efforts. They are simply a means to an end; a way of leveraging the functional logic. This logic is based on economic objectives and serves to add value, improve results, increase productivity, raise effectiveness, ensure labour efficiency and eliminate deficits.

From the client's perspective, this approach has a number of strengths: it helps overcome crises, offers excellent ideas, is based on real business contexts, is measurable, uses words the client understands and, above all, offers certainty in an uncertain situation. "They can do the things we can't do ourselves." "We know what we'll be getting for our money."

In contrast, optimizing communication processes within and between organisations and their stakeholders is a central issue in *systemic process consulting*. Introducing transparency into patterns of thought and action ultimately helps an organisation to define its own goals, develop shared values, clarify expectations and reach agreement on how best to implement its plans. Systemic organisational consulting sees and treats an organisation as a living organism with the ability and power to develop its own solutions to difficult situations and problems. This approach uses carefully selected interventions to help the organisation release blocked energies, reach joint agreements in shared decision-making processes and determine how best to achieve its stated goals.

Ultimately, both approaches aim to help their clients become more successful; they just have very different ways of doing so.

Systemic process consulting is highly context-oriented, takes a more open attitude to results and individual process steps, involves those directly affected by the situation and mobilises energy. However, it also requires reflection and feedback processes. As a result, it initially produces more uncertainty than certainty. The identification of internal patterns of thought and action, a deeper understanding of how problems arise and an improved ability to communicate and solve problems means that sustainable solutions emerge for the company almost of their own accord. However, systemic process consultants must take care to maintain an appropriate distance to the client system to ensure any "blind spots" are noticed.

Business process consultants often think and act in a similar manner to the client. They install themselves on site within the client system and can therefore be consulted directly, make concrete suggestions and participate in decision-making processes. The implementation of any proposed measures is left to the client.

A further significant difference between traditional business process and systemic process consulting lies in the circumstances and conditions that lead to the selection of a particular approach.

Since systemic consulting ultimately looks to introduce longer-term, sustainable change, organisations that find themselves facing a crisis that threatens their immediate survival generally call in the business process consultants first. Their hope is that the consultants will provide them with the necessary decision-making basis they seek and recommend short-term measures that will have immediate effect. In times of economic stagnation or depression, when longer-term, positive expectations are overshadowed by more pressing worries about the immediate future, people often lack the time, understanding and insight to think about longer-term, sustainable development. Consequently, the actual needs and expectations of the client system also determine the choice of consulting approach: forceful, clear, profit-oriented, "top-down" measures versus the impetus and motivation to concentrate and reflect on inherent strengths and powers.

In some cases, companies might just be seeking an "alibi", i.e. looking to hide behind the reputation of a large consulting firm and using its recommendations to endorse the need for the consulting process itself and/or any unpopular measures that might need to be implemented.

Interest in the systemic approach often stems either from some form of prior knowledge, understanding or practical experience of process consulting, from publications on the subject or through a personal recommendation or contact. Any such background influences not only the project acquisition activities, but also the setting for the initial meeting, mutual expectations, contractual negotiations and the client-consultant relationship.

In this sense, not only does each approach get the clients who suit it best, each client also gets the best form of consulting for its particular situation.

3. Does a Combined Approach Offer Added Value for Clients?

In *Faust II* Goethe already differentiates between the *what* and the *how* in the Laboratory Scene, when Homunculus proclaims, "*Ponder the What – to solve the How still harder try.*"

In less poetic terms, this means that each *what* creates a *how* and each *how* is the *what* in the next step. In an integrative consulting approach, the problem is no longer split into a *what* (business process consulting) and a *how* (systemic process consulting). Instead, professional, business-related issues are embedded from the start in an appropriate systemic process architecture. The client only deals with one (joint) consultant system and can monitor corporate development as a whole; the links between strategy, structure and culture, between market share, profit margins and other goals are brought together in one single, unified concept. A combined approach offers many benefits for the client, the four most important of which are:

- *Independent problem-solving competence and sustainability*: an integrated development process raises awareness and broadens and strengthens the client system's ability to solve problems. The transfer of know-how then follows on implicitly, and clients are soon able to apply the systemic process skills needed to steer their organisations and develop the necessary business process skills without external support. Companies who reflect carefully on situations of conflict are generally more responsive and receptive to their environments. They adapt better to unforeseen market developments, develop stable early warning systems and deal more quickly and efficiently with any crises that emerge. By becoming "fit for the future", companies can transform themselves from followers into leaders and develop the strengths they need to move beyond what they thought were their previous limits.
- *Reaching goals more easily*: in an integrated approach, the design and implementation phases take place simultaneously, not consecutively. The way plans are made and implemented at this early stage, and the people involved, play an important role, since this is where the impetus is set and the attainability of short and long-term goals is gauged and assessed. Many companies have now come to realise that no matter how good a concept might be, it will be of little use if they do not actively promote it and actually do something with it. Only an integrated consulting approach can lead to lasting, forward-looking change: it does not treat organisations like submissive patients who need to be told what medicine to take, but instead encourages them to develop their own powers of self-healing.
- *Easing the (internal) potential for conflict*: the conflicting paradigms found in the two approaches (and in the client system itself) can be a major source of conflict and usually become most apparent when under pressure. In an integrated consultant system, these paradigms are pre-prepared to perfection and all but pre-digested, thus making them far easier to then reconcile in the client system. The contradictions, differences and advantages of the two approaches are jointly reflected upon by all concerned and the results presented in the form of integrated interventions. In this way, the short-term relief realised through the business-consulting measures combines with the long-term

support of systemic consulting to produce the best possible overall effects.
- *Building a reputation through social responsibility*: companies assume a high degree of social responsibility and make significant contributions to economic prosperity and the quality of life. They create jobs and influence politics, education and the Arts. Companies who opt for an integrated approach are characterised by greater public visibility and market penetration. This social responsibility is apparent in the impetus it gives to the discourse on socio-relevant issues such as the future of work, lifelong learning, the new corporate role in society, the link between sustainability and prosperity, ethics, etc.

4. Systemic Integrative Consulting – A New Business Model?

Although we have many years of practical experience with integrated consulting projects, we are still elaborating a model that does justice to the complexity of an integrated approach to change processes. In our book on systemic integration management (Königswieser et al. 2001, p. 53), we introduced a model that illustrates the work carried out simultaneously on the professional, content-related and process levels, which is based on four key factors (structure, culture, strategy and vision) in development processes. The loop between the present and the vision for the future is represented by the continual "systemic reflective loop". This, in turn, contains the following four iterative steps: gathering information, building hypotheses, planning interventions and intervention (see section 3).

Although this model takes the combination of hard and soft factors and of systemic process and business-process consulting into account, it by no means integrates them fully or sufficiently. We have held many discussions and learning workshops with experts and colleagues[2] to try to develop an extended version of this model, a version that can be seen as a "work in progress". Fig. 1 shows an example of one such possible draft model.

2 In addition to the authors, the following colleagues participated in these learning workshops: Uwe Cichy, Uwe Dahl, Gerhard Jochum, Ulrich Königswieser, Erik Lang, Christian Matul, Peter Panholzer, Patricia Van Overstraeten.

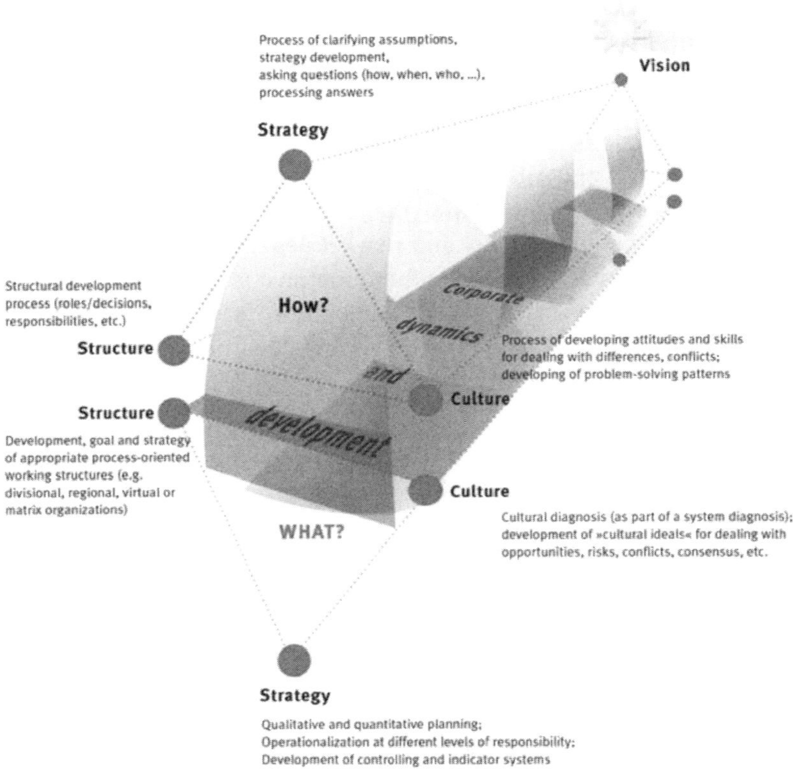

Figure 1: SIM2

In our deliberations, we have assumed that much of what really goes on in corporate dynamics is the result of the interaction between and the interspersing of the *whats* and the *hows* in strategy, structure and culture. After all, the *what* cannot be separated from the *how*; they are dependent on and constantly interact with each other.

If business process consulting traditionally concentrates on the *what*, then its systemic counterpart focuses on the *how*. Consequently, as stand-alone solutions, neither can really do proper justice to the issues of corporate dynamics and development, even if an abstractive approach and way of looking at the situation might sometimes seem necessary to reduce complexity.

Depending on the situation and its requirements and needs, consulting processes based on this model vary their interventions between the dimensions in the triangles, without turning them into a uniform mishmash and blurring their limits, yet still introducing a new level of quality. The reflection loops form the links and are closely interwoven with corporate dynamics and development.

In fact, in the real and chaotic world, it is this depth of perception which highlights some aspects and hides others, without letting them disappear entirely from view. When we zoom in on one specific dimension, we can only see the others out of the corner of our eye. Changing the focus opens up the expanse and reveals the other aspects. Specializing in one aspect allows us to develop excellence and depth without losing sight of the bigger picture.

Complementarity theory (cf. Ruigrok 2000) also confirms a disparately high probability of economic success when a simultaneous and complementary approach to development processes results in the establishment of a positive, self-influencing feedback loop.

The reflective aspect inherent in the systemic loop is an indispensable element in a combined consulting approach. At the initial meeting with the client, it serves to establish a basic assessment of any manifest and latent issues that might be affecting the client system, an assessment which will later influence the choice of consulting staff, the project goals, the priorities set and the methods chosen.

This reflective meta-communication between the business and systemic process consultants remains an essential component throughout the entire consulting process, from the initial diagnosis, through to the project milestones and the ongoing discussions that take place with the client and in the consulting team. It is through this ongoing communication that any previously unnoticed incompatibilities will ultimately be revealed. If this reflective element does not become a matter of course in a mixed consulting team, our experience shows that the combined energies in this team will not be released.

Hand in hand with the reflective, discursive clarification of the effect of interventions comes a further process element, namely feedback. This includes the feedback processes both within the combined consulting team, between the individual units in the client system and between the client system and the consultants. It is important to ensure that sufficient time and space is given to this form of communication and that it is seen and understood by all as a self-organizing process of learning.

The fascination of this "twin turbo consulting", as one colleague neatly put it, lies not in the theory, but in the actual consulting activities themselves. These require a shared understanding of project goals, concurrence on procedures, compatible values and a general setting and framework that can accommodate the process ideals behind this model.

If the common goals of an integrated consulting approach are a sustained, qualitative increase in the available options for action coupled with greater "mindfulness" (cf. Weick and Sutcliffe 2004) and greater success for the client in its business activities, then it is the "attitude" adopted by all the consultants involved that makes such an approach work (see section 3). "Attitude" is the way we relate to ourselves, our colleagues, our clients and our general environment; it is the way we think. It controls our categories of perception, ways of doing things, priorities, intervention strategies, limits and conditions.

5. An Integrative Approach to Consulting

Integrated consulting works best and produces the most professional results when representatives of both approaches work together either in tandem or as members of a mixed team. Of course, this is only possible if the team members on both sides are familiar with the tasks, goals, methods and mental models used in the alternative approach and everyone is prepared to look at organisational development from a unified perspective.

This approach provides access to know-how from both fields, which can then be turned into hypotheses and applied as required to suit the actual context and situation. Business process know-how is thus used not to set and plan requirements, but to ask the kind of questions that will eventually lead to solutions. In other words, business process consultants act as expert sparring partners for their systemic process counterparts, adding a further option to proposed solutions and opening up new ways of looking at innovative measures.

Combining this aspect with systemic process know-how means that the effects of any planned interventions at the architecture, design and tools levels are constantly reflected upon and adapted as required to suit the process. This process of professional reflection is a central element in the model and produces a qualitatively different view of the issues. The more intelligent use of expertise and analytical planning strengths that comes with the addition of the process focus simply enhances their existing strengths. For example, cost-cutting measures are far easier to sustain if their effects are considered and the people they affect are involved in the decision-making process.

The use of reflection loops and self-observation techniques helps companies to develop new ways of looking at their own organisation. This, in turn, equips them with new ways of steering the organisation and new problem-solving patterns. The model also allows the consulting team to intervene in extreme situations and share in the work of dealing with a difficult problem.

One of the key elements in this model is its flexibility: it enables consultants to respond to a specific situation and opt for the type of know-how that bests fits current gaps. What is "right" for one company might just as easily be "wrong" in another. Like managers, who have to adapt their behaviour to compensate for the specifics of a given situation, consultants who work with this approach leverage the actual level of development in the client system.

Developing a relationship of trust with the client is particularly important in an integrated consulting model. After all, client expectations play a decisive role in the process. If a client expects and demands security, clarity, decision-making support, expertise and a constant on-site consultant presence, a cautious process of persuasion will have to be initiated to encourage them to change their outlook and venture into an unsettling reflection process. In such cases, the systemic consultants will initially have to assume a coaching role to guarantee the desired outcome.

Proximity and distance have different, yet equally valid functions in each of the two approaches. Business process consultants are actively involved in operations and have to provide the client with support in day-to-day business activities. Their presence is required on site. Systemic process consultants, on the other hand, can only properly fulfil their task if they maintain a healthy distance, provide an external perspective, intervene as required but then withdraw again to avoid endangering the autonomy of the client system.

As a result, coordinating a tandem or team-based integrated consulting project is no easy task and must above all factor in a considerable amount of time on top of any on-site consulting activities for joint reflection.

All these issues serve to shape the profile of a suitable "candidate" for integrated consulting. In addition to business or systemic process know-how, an integrated consultant must also exhibit a certain degree of maturity. This does not mean they have to be absolutely perfect; it simply means they must be able to accommodate their own strengths and weaknesses – and those of others – in a reflected and deliberate manner. This is generally referred to as "social competence".

6. The Main Challenges and Difficulties of a Combined Approach

The theory sounds relatively simple: bring together, combine and integrate different types of knowledge and expertise for the good of the client. But, in fact, practice shows it to be an extremely difficult, often almost impossible undertaking, even if the client has expressly requested an integrated approach. So why should this be the case? Based on our experience, we can offer the following three explanations:

"The differences are too great"

Business and systemic process consultants base their work on different theoretical models, constructions of reality and values. They represent two contrary schools of thought. The specific competences available to each of the two approaches, the way they are applied and the purpose that they serve are rooted in different, often contradictory basic assumptions. True integration would only be possible if either business process consulting were to drop its linearity and rational unity or systemic process consulting were to give up its openness and assumption of complexity. In other words, both approaches would have to either dissociate themselves from or reassess and redevelop their basic assumptions. In our personal encounters with representatives of large, traditional consulting firms who had invited us to take part in joint projects, we observed a similar set of fears on both sides. Both are stunned by the huge and unsettling differences that separate them and threaten their individual identities. They put each other down to protect their own identities and territories. Sutrich (2003) refers in this context not only to the "new horizons" appearing on the consulting scene, but also to the inhabitants of two different groups of islands – history made them arch enemies and they still keep up this tradition today.

"This is pioneering work; it needs to be tried, tested and learned."
Since the underlying paradigms, models and experiences behind each approach are so different, the motivation behind any attempts to address the challenge of integrating them has to be very strong. Nonetheless, before any such attempt can be made, both sides have to first acquire a basic understanding of what their counterparts do and how they achieve it. There is a far greater risk of competition ("Who is better?"), power struggles ("Who has a stronger influence on the client system?") and identity crises ("Which approach does the client seem to prefer?") in a "mixed" consulting team than there is in a homogenous one. If the members of such a team do not accept each other, if they can't adopt an attitude of complementarity, if they are not flexible enough to swap the "lead" to suit the actual situation or willing to vary their approach as required, any attempts at cooperation will falter at the first hurdle, i.e. at the first sign of criticism from the client.

"Without the necessary structural framework, it simply won't work."
Even if the relationship between the tandem partners can withstand the strain and everyone sees and accepts the differences between the two approaches as a valuable resource, successful cooperation still needs an appropriate framework and conditions if it is to work.

7. Case Studies

The following case studies illustrate some of the practical issues facing an integrated consulting business model. They were chosen both for the insights they offer into positive (successful) and negative (unsuccessful) projects alike, as well as for the valuable lessons that can be learned from them.

7.1 Project A (Terminated)

Background

A leading automobile parts supplier had decided to extend its portfolio to include the development of complete vehicles and the construction of niche vehicles. To do so, the supplier had already acquired another company specialised in the field of automobile development. They approached us and enquired about specialist coaching for setting up an automobile manufacturing plant. The contact came through one of our partners, who had extensive knowledge and experience of the automobile industry.

In our initial meetings with the client, we signalled the complexity of the situation and drew their attention to the fact that business process consulting alone would not satisfy their requirements and address the impact of the impending change process. The two companies had very different cultures: one was a manual, manufacturing environment, the other a creative, development organisation.

Project Goals

Company management saw no need for additional systemic coaching: all they wanted to do was build their manufacturing plant. They did not feel coaching or guidance would facilitate the integration process. After all, "Plenty of other manufacturing companies have been successfully integrated in the past without the help of consultants." However, when they realised that they could only have the business process consulting if they agreed to combine it with systemic consulting for the entire change process, they somewhat reluctantly gave their consent.

Architecture/Design

We proposed a process architecture and began with a system diagnosis. The results of this diagnosis were used to build a set of hypotheses, which were then presented to company management and used to determine the starting points for the consulting process. A steering group was set up and defined a number of sub-projects to address particular individual areas where improvement was required.

We considered the "Planning the Manufacturing Plant" sub-project to be an integral part of the whole change process, since once completed it would lead to a re-orientation of the entire company. As a result, we proposed that the leader of the "Vehicle Manufacturing" sub-project should also be included in the steering group. But this proposal was rejected by management on the grounds that they needed to produce rapid results if they were going to win new projects. The sub-projects therefore ran in parallel, with no attempts to cross-reference results.

After a second "sounding board" session, the clients decided they no longer required a combined consulting approach in their integration process. We were asked to moderate future workshops, but we would no longer be able to steer the entire process. We declined this new arrangement: for us the project was effectively over.

Results

The "Vehicle Manufacturing" project had by then reached the stage where it was ready to hold initial discussions with potential clients. However, a subsequent slump in the automobile industry coupled with an economic downturn in the company, led to the project being shelved.

Lessons Learned

One of the major problems in this project was the fact that the two different forms of consulting were "bought" as separate entities and therefore ran alongside each other from the start. The business process approach was pushed into the leading role, while the significance of systemic process consulting and its purpose in the development process was kept deliberately vague and undervalued. Consequently, no coordination of efforts and synergies between the two approaches was possible. The client accepted neither the need for an integrated approach nor, for that matter, a systemic approach at all. This highlights the importance of a joint approach and consensus for the planning and definition of projects of this kind. If the client neither appreciates nor embraces an integrated approach, it will be doomed to fail from the outset.

7.2 Project B (successful)

Background

A subsidiary of a large, German industrial group was facing difficult times. Its market share was decreasing, its quality levels no longer met customer expectations and high production costs made it increasingly uncompetitive. It had already undergone a long-term cost cutting programme, which had succeeded in returning the company to profit, but the programme had also clearly left its mark on the organisation: the workforce was not motivated and staff turnover was high.

Project Goals

Management decided to initiate a change process that it hoped would turn the company into the industry leader in terms of price and quality. They engaged the services of the consulting firm they felt was best equipped to implement this change process. We were asked to provide support and coaching for the "Production" division.

The change process in the Production division was led by two senior consultants, one from a traditional consulting background, the other with systemic know-how and expertise. A further five consultants were also involved in this part of the project.

Architecture/Design

The company had already decided to introduce a new production system and, since their US-based parent company had also recently introduced such a system, they felt it would be advantageous to use the same one. However, the system could not simply be implemented as it was: some customisation was needed to address both cultural differences and local technical constraints. Introducing a production system of this kind would mean a complete change in workflows and the way things were done – both at management and grassroots level. Basically, they were trying to introduce more teamwork, to delegate responsibility for quality and productivity and create awareness of the need for discipline and standard procedures. A targets system that took into consideration both hard and soft factors was also developed and integrated into a balanced scorecard.

The architecture agreed upon for this project allowed people both to contribute to and at the same time learn about the new production system. When the system was later introduced across all manufacturing plants, what had been learned in this initial phase was then passed on to the remaining 17,000 employees using a cascade process.

The first step in the change process was again the formation of a steering group, this time chaired by the Member of the Board responsible for Production. The steering group also included individual plant managers and representatives of the central divisions. It was coached by two consultants (one from each of the approaches).

The production system envisaged five sub-systems, each aimed at a specific aspect. It also included over one hundred individual tools. The steering group's first task was to define the new production system and sub-systems in greater detail and allocate the necessary tools.

Five working groups were then formed to work on the concepts planned for each individual sub-system. They were each to produce a manual explaining the effects and interaction between the various processes in clear and concise terms; a task which took around four months. These interdisciplinary working groups also included representatives of each of the individual plants, thus ensuring that the acquired know-how would later be available at a local level. Work began with a kick-off meeting to present and discuss aims and objectives.

In this phase, progress was presented to the steering group at four-week intervals; any open issues were discussed and resolved in these meetings. Weekly telephone conferences were held between the consultants and the sub-project leaders to clarify and define the links between the individual projects.

Once the manuals were ready, a workshop lasting several days was organised for all involved to communicate what had been learned in the working groups. Implementation teams were formed for each plant, each made up entirely of local staff involved in the conceptual phase. Pilot areas were selected for the introduction of the system in the plants.

Results

The first measurable effects were achieved within a very short period of time. Quality levels improved tremendously. The system was subsequently introduced company-wide.

Lessons Learned

One factor in the successful completion of this project was the fact that the systemic and business process consultants worked together harmoniously from the outset. The client was not really aware of any differences between the two approaches during the actual consulting process. Any decisions on what, when and how things were to be done were taken jointly by the entire consulting team. Both sides had a good understanding of the other approach and respected each other's work. Some additional factors that contributed to its success included: mutual acceptance of the agreed architecture; the definition and implementation of the process by the clients themselves with the support of the systemic process consultants (an approach the business process consultants found quite unusual) and the parallel coaching for the management team.

7.3 Project C (successful)

Background

The client for this project is a highly profitable Swiss company, which enjoys near-monopoly status in the country's retail market and is regarded almost as a national icon in Switzerland. However, its cooperative-like structure and high vertical integration also brought with them a decentralised autonomy, complicated cost structures and slow decision-making processes. Changes were urgently needed if the company was to retain its leading position in an increasingly competitive market. The situation boded well for a combined approach: our sponsor in the largest division (Purchasing and Marketing) was a holistically-minded, highly respected manager, while the project leader was a systems thinking-oriented "doer" with a strong influence on the choice of the consultants.

Project Goals

- To introduce a competitive, efficient, forward-looking structure: the company should retain its leading position in the home market and, at the same time, expand its international activities.
- To develop a strategic vision that reflected the new corporate self-image.
- To cut costs by 15 % and increase efficiency by 20 %.
- To introduce a culture of empowerment and develop the competences required both at a corporate and at a personal/role level to reach these ambitious goals.
- To bring about a change in mentality and attitude amongst all employees.

Architecture/Design

A system diagnosis (addressing professional and cultural issues) was carried out using group interviews and other analysis forms. The results of this diagnosis were mirrored to key corporate players in a two-day workshop. The conclusion: a great, friendly company that nonetheless demonstrated a tendency to bury its head in the sand with regard to the future.

Goals were agreed and set in cooperation with the clients, the process architecture was defined and the following sub-projects agreed upon: structure, cost-cutting potential, identity and leadership. Six months down the line, when it became apparent that the goals could not be achieved without job losses, a further sub-project was added: dealing with uncertainty and change.

The sub-project leaders met every four weeks in the steering group, which was made up of representatives of all – nine at the time – hierarchical levels. Two members of the six-person consulting team (three business and three systemic process consultants) coached and guided the steering group, the project group and the conflict-ridden sponsor group. The groups were very motivated and the feedback they received was positive: they were "doing a great job"; their work was courageous, innovative and taboo-breaking yet mindful of corporate culture and identity. The consulting team provided support in the form of scenarios and decision-making options and introduced reflection loops not only in its own deliberations, but also in its work with the client, thus reducing blind spots, raising awareness and heightening alertness.

One peculiarity of this project was the involvement of a group of "special experts" from an international consulting firm. They had been given a very specific brief and allocated very specific roles (e.g. calculating models) by top management, a fact that, as it later transpired, had somewhat "hurt their pride". Consequently, they found it difficult to cooperate with us as process leaders and coordinators and were very critical and dismissive of the whole process, commenting at one stage, "The groups will never make it without our help." But make it they did. Our particular role was "limited" to professional and process coaching and guidance.

Results

Over a twelve-month period, the company underwent a process of radical systemic change. Of the nine original hierarchical levels, only six remained. Efficiency was indeed increased by an estimated 20 %. Cost-cutting measures were identified to achieve the targeted 15 % in savings, with more in reserve for further investments. The workforce was reduced by 10 %. Everyone faced and dealt with their grief, anger and uncertainty together. The process of changing mentalities and attitudes is still ongoing.

Lessons Learned

This project highlights the importance of co-development and a good understanding of the chosen approach on the part of the client. In this case, both the project leaders and the sponsors supported the integrated approach and were convinced of its benefits from the start. The consultants and clients worked together to co-develop the project. The mixed consulting team, whose members all shared a similar mindset, trusted and respected each other and were very motivated by the prospect of developing this model further. As a consulting team, we also benefited greatly from the inclusion of a supervision for our own work and an evaluation of our own processes during the project. However, we had not expected to encounter such a feeling of mistrust and lack of respect from the "special experts". Despite all our best efforts, we were unable to establish any common ground.

8. Critical Success Factors

There are many aspects that contribute to the success of an integrated approach to organisational consulting. Based on our own practical experience and drawing on the conclusions of the research reports based on our consulting projects (e.g. Froschauer and Lueger 2003), we would like to draw particular attention to the following critical success factors:

- Mutual acceptance and respect
- Basic know-how of both approaches
- Common values
- A reflective approach to consulting activities
- Seamless transitions to suit the individual situation.

These success factors have, in turn, helped us to determine the main conditions that we feel have to be met to ensure the success of an integrated consulting project:

1. A clear contract must be established with the client system, which defines expectations and sets them as goals that are clearly understood by all concerned.
2. The client must be in favour of an integrated approach and recognise the added value it provides (method and effect).
3. The project must be carried out in close collaboration with internal experts and involve the people who will be affected by the change.
4. Relevant stakeholders and interest groups (e.g. customers, shareholders, management, suppliers, employees) must be involved in the project, and there must be a constant review of the correlation between process decisions and economic aspects (benchmarking).
5. Professional expertise should be made available if required (what, when, how much, where development is needed, where to implement change).

6. Any decisions made and their consequences must be clear to all concerned.
7. Reflection loops should become standard practice.
8. Consultants must work in close collaboration with the project leaders who, in turn, recognise and personify the logic behind such an integrated approach.
9. The project must be based on an architecture that inspires confidence and facilitates dealing with uncertainty.
10. The work carried out by the consulting staff must be of a high quality and must factor in enough time and capacity for reflection, for decisions concerning any interventions, for supervision. Responsibility for the project as a whole must also, of course, be shared by all concerned.

It will still take some time for this integrated model to reach maturity, for clear concepts and terminology to emerge and for the design principles to evolve and become communicable. After all, it is very much a work in progress. This article is intended merely as an interim report, a contribution to the discourse.

9. References

Froschauer, U. & Lueger, M. (2003): Reflective-differentiating Consulting. Reflections on Combining Systemic Process and Business Process Consulting. Vienna: Unpublished Research Report.

Königswieser, R., Cichy, U., Jochum, G. (2001): SIMsalabim. Veränderung ist keine Zauberei. SystemischesIntegrationsManagement. Stuttgart: Klett-Cotta

Mohe, M. & Heinecke, M. J. (Eds.) (2002): Consulting Problemlösung als Geschäftsmodell. Stuttgart: Klett-Cotta

Peters, T. & Waterman, R. (1982): In Search of Excellence: Lessons from America's Best-Run Companies. New York: Harper & Row.

Ruigrok, W. (2000): Komplementaritäten. *GDI-Impuls* 2: 49 ff.

Sutrich, O (2003): Neuland für junge Berater am Horizont. *Profile* 5: 53–65

Weick, K, E. & Sutcliffe, K. E. (2001): Managing the Unexpected: Assuring High Performance in an Age of Complexity. San Francisco: Jossey-Bass.

Zech, R. (2004): Rat und Unrat. Eine kleine Reflexion über Beratung. In: Grosz, A. & Witt, J. (Eds.): Living at Work. Munich/Vienna: Hanser.

About the Authors

Roswita Königswieser, Königswieser & Network Systemische Beratung und Entwicklung GmbH, Vienna. Focus: systemic consulting in international organisations; integration of business process and systemic process consulting; scientific research and publications; executive coaching; training for change managers and consultants.

Martin Hillebrand, Königswieser & Network Systemische Beratung und Entwicklung GmbH, Bremen. Focus: design and coaching for complex, sustainable change processes; implementation of strategies for planning, target agreements and remuneration systems; training for change managers and consultants.